IN TO

CU01456418

"101 Secrets of highly successful,
fun businesses"

John Laithwaite - Stuart Wilkinson

Foreword by Matt Roberts
Illustrations by Jim Rennert

Dedicated to
Yvette, Danik, Alexandra and Christian

Contents

vi GETTING YOUR MESSAGE TO MARKET

Foreword

Why write a book? It's certainly not aimed at being a best-seller. Stuart and I came up with the idea after advising Coinamatic of Canada how we ran our unique, incredible, exciting and highly successful business. In talking at this meeting, and at three or four subsequent meetings educating other successful companies from all over the world, we decided that we wanted to share with a wider audience some of the reasons for our phenomenal success.

When I started the business did I have a vision? No! Did I want to make millions? No!

Yes, make some money, but I always wanted independence and to prove that I could be successful working for myself. I wanted to win, to be the best but do it fairly, to work with like-minded people, build a team to share in the highs and lows and to reward success.

Before finishing my A-levels and without a degree, I started my 'career' in a bank. I gained knowledge of how to borrow money, and met my lovely wife and future business partner who was a customer of the bank, and a very careful saver. I left the bank aged 22 having earned respect from my boss Neil Meyer who, four years later, lent me £2,000 to start JLA.

In 1966, I started work as a Service Engineer for my dad. I agreed on the condition that, during my first year, I would learn how to fix machines and he would teach me the business so that I could take over his role. I was paid £30 per week but found it quite boring running retail laundry stores. What I enjoyed was buying fifty machines when we only needed ten. In the event, I sold the other forty machines at a good mark-up. I started buying new and used machines, using a few in our shops and selling off the rest. I loved the cut and thrust of buying and selling. My dad had a very unambitious business partner who blocked most expansion ideas. He wouldn't agree to me getting a bonus for my efforts, and suggested that I start on my own. My dad told me to deal in machines outside the business, so I left and JLA was born.

My Replacement

I started to look for my replacement at JLA from day one but only found him when Stuart walked into my office seventeen years later. We became instant friends and two years later, I persuaded him to join JLA as my number two. In the following years, this developed into brilliant partnership that has lasted over twenty years. In many ways we are opposites, but have an ability to complement each other's talents and also to cover for our individual weaknesses.

Stuart started with JLA as Deputy Managing Director. He worked in all aspects of business; in operations, sales and finance before becoming Managing Director and finally Chief Executive Officer. Together we built JLA into the most successful laundry equipment sales and rental business in the world.

We built a great team to take the business on to new levels. We shared so much fun and laughter, ups and downs and had a team always ten steps ahead, always in touch.

Internationally, I was the name and the face of JLA but Stuart was always there keeping the business moving forward. With Stuart's talent, his pure hard work and his compassion, we built a phenomenal team, and together we became trusted by customers, loved and respected by suppliers, and feared by competitors.

Together we built an exceptionally successful business but we did it with compassion. 37 years later, I have never regretted a minute. It was living life to the full, with laughs and success all the way.

The JLA business model was very capital-intensive. Each year, we had fantastic success. The more we grew, the more investment we needed and the more discussions we had to have with banks that didn't understand our business.

Eventually ground down by banks, I sold JLA in 2010 to a private equity firm.

Still IN TOUCH

After we sold JLA, I stayed on as chairman and signed up for three years. Unfortunately the new management style clashed with how Stuart and I had enjoyed running the company, and we parted ways after ten months.

Leaving gave me the chance to enjoy exploring new and challenging investment opportunities - some through institutional investments and some directly. All were with great people with great ideas but some lacked good financial control and management.

My motivation was never to run these businesses but always to bring my experience, successes and failures to help a new generation of entrepreneurs and businessmen to be the best they could be.

I did this in two laundry businesses that I knew well in China and Germany; both have gone from strength to strength and are now large, successful companies.

In 2014 a great new chapter in my business life came from a brilliant decision I made to invest in Non Executive Directors. com. I joined Ian Wright the founder and we quickly recruited Matt Roberts as CEO. The speed of development has been phenomenal.

We started with 4 people in January and moved from our small remote office in Lancashire to the heart of the business district in Manchester. The business immediately took off. Over the next 2 years we introduced new networks and eventually had to move premises to a very convenient and beautiful building, The Peninsula, next to Victoria Station and the transport hub of Manchester.

Ian, who had had the initial unique idea, decided at the time to move on, so Matt and I became the two partners owning the business. We decided to change the company name to

In Touch Networks, probably the only time a business was named after a book! In fact, the book illustrates so many principles that resonate throughout the business.

Success has followed success. We now employ over 100 people, our offices have expanded to 11,000 square feet in The Peninsula, and since January 2015 the business has grown by 1400%. In November 2016 we were the fastest-growing tech business in the North West in the Deloitte Fast 50 awards.

We now plan to open our US office in Charlotte, NC, in the early part of 2017.

Today I get the same buzz, thrill and enjoyment with In Touch Networks as any that I have had in my business career to date. I hope some of the passion, drive and success that I have, and still experience today, is evident in this book and helps you to make even a small positive change to your own business experience in the future.

John Laithwaite

Matt Roberts Foreword

Choosing what to say in this foreword is a difficult task. I could write pages on John's character, or on his extensive expertise and accomplishments. Or it could serve as a testimonial, because the guiding principles set out in this book have made In Touch Networks the success it is today. Instead, I'll explain how John's insight – which you now hold neatly packaged in your hands – has powerfully impacted my own business and thinking.

My friendship with John very nearly didn't happen. Ian Wright, the founder of Non-Executive Directors, which is now In Touch Networks, headhunted me for an amazing position with a large global company while he was simultaneously trying to get NonExecutiveDirectors.com off the ground. Ian and I got on immediately and he showed me this unbelievable online business he had created which needed "turbocharging". John Laithwaite had recently bought 50% of this business and Ian arranged for us to meet.

I met John in the Malmaison bar in Manchester city centre. That meeting set the tone of our working relationship from day one – John had arranged to meet me at 1pm, but called me at 12 to say he had arrived. I quickly jumped in my car and sped to Manchester - already following the advice of one of this book's chapters, 'The bus is in town'. Too many opportunities are missed every day by indecision and delay, and I'm pleased to say my meeting with John wasn't one of them.

John explained that the business was based in a tiny office in Preston with one part-time member of staff. Ian didn't want to expose the business to too much 'cost' in the early stages, and therefore asked me to do two days per week (which can be roughly translated to "full-time, but I don't want to pay you!"). Ultimately, this wasn't about the money, this was about how much I loved the business, and the lessons in this book show how vital this approach is.

I immediately got on immensely well with John. Although his first business, JLA, was about as far from my background in digital marketing as humanly possible, all his principles, knowledge and lessons were aligned perfectly with my approach to business.

The fundamental propositions and practices in these pages have provided consistent guidance throughout the journey of In Touch Networks.

Day one was all about data – the lifeblood of any business, and we had lots of it. We needed a way of speaking with our online customers and our success fundamentally came from telesales - the backbone of JLA and what has become the backbone of In Touch Networks. We knew we had to understand each type of customer and deal with them individually – our demographic wasn't and isn't the tech generation. Our customers like speaking with people, engaging with them, and receiving a personal service. This unique combination of online and telephone is exactly what has made our business what it is today.

Why is In Touch Networks so successful? The answer is because it was an amazing idea, delivered by a fantastic team and backed up by John's inspiring guidance and business knowledge. John hasn't given me a set of rules, rather a cultural mindset for our business. All of the lessons I take from John are laid out in these pages – run your business daily, build a team, look after your staff, plan to succeed, hire people with passion, run your business like you are never going to sell and if something is working well, break it and fix it better!

It is our relationship, these principles and the team that have grown our business by 1500% inside two years.

John has an unbelievable ability to explain things in a way that just make sense. You can apply most chapters in this book to your business, so don't wait for the bus to leave town. DO IT NOW!

Matt Roberts
CEO – In Touch Networks

About the Artist - Jim Rennert

We'd like to personally thank the talented Jim Rennert for illustrating the book. Jim is an exceptional artist, sculptor and friend. I have a sculpture of his, titled Teamwork, at home and chose it as the image on the book's front cover.

When I asked permission to use this as the book's cover and Jim requested a copy of the book, I happily obliged. I was pleased to hear Jim enjoyed the book, but was even more bowled over when he agreed to replace the original cartoon illustrations with a mix of bespoke and existing images to bring the stories to life.

Jim started sculpting in 1990, after ten years of working in business, and his art has graced galleries across the United States, so it is a real honour to have the same works grace these pages.

Jim's work is figurative, emphasising movement and action - a key theme of the book - and his business background influenced many of the pieces in the book, which form a collection called "Suits".

Stuart and I were drawn to the humour of Jim's pieces in the book, depicting the daily ups and downs of business life, and love how they match up perfectly to the chapters.

To see more of Jim's work, please visit www.jimrennert.com or www.cavaliergalleries.com, and to discuss a purchase or a commission, please contact Jim's agent, Ron Cavalier at art@cavaliergalleries.com.

ESSENCE

In 2000, Dick Cardis and I had learnt the importance of brands but weren't sure if 'JLA' was the brand we should move forward with. We contracted The Attic, a worldwide brand agency with their Head Office in Yorkshire, to advise us. They interviewed hundreds of customers, suppliers, competitors and staff to get the essence of JLA.

The result was not to change the brand as it was so warm and respected and had such a great feeling about it. So they cleaned the lettering, gave us a 'swoosh' and we kept 'JLA'. Equally important as the brand, they also confirmed the core values of the business, the five words which became the essence of JLA:

1. In touch

2. Open

3. Action

4. Flexible

5. Passion

These are as relevant now as they were in 2000.

In touch

1   In touch

The first rule of this book is 'In touch'. Stuart, Sue and I feel that this phrase epitomises what was great about JLA.

The industry - In touch
Sue and I travelled all over the world to seminars, conventions and exhibitions, and to visit all of the suppliers; current ones, future ones and never-consider ones.

We visited other distributors, installations, coin laundries and manufacturers. We were in touch.

All of the sales staff were encouraged to go to hotel exhibitions and conventions run by care home associations, universities and medical organisations. Our key account people were in touch with the industry they supplied. Know your customer.

Staff - In touch
Most importantly, stay in touch with your staff. Stuart and I had 'In Touch' meetings all over the country. Short presentations followed by questions, then food and socialising. The table layout was nightclub-style so the management could wander from table to table to chat with all of the staff. We were definitely in touch.

Whether it is a company newsletter, informal or formal meetings, annual conferences or one-to-one, any excuse to celebrate success, keeping everyone informed is good management.

In touch

Open

2   Open

One of our strong principles was to be as open as possible with staff, suppliers and customers.

If you saw our offices, they were open-plan. Around the periphery were glass offices, in which were most of the top management team including Stuart and myself. Yes, we could see out and what was going on in sales and operations, but also, all of our staff could see that we were there and what we were doing. If the doors to our offices were open, it was an encouragement for people to walk in.

We had giant screens all over the office, all over the walls telling everyone how sales were going and the number of appointments in the week, debts collected, what parts we had sold, and a map of where Service Engineers were at any one time.

We shared with the staff all targets and budgets, and how the company was doing financially. There are many other examples, too many to list, but the principle was to be open with staff, suppliers and customers.

Open

3   Action

Nothing in business stands still. It is better to take immediate action when you are aware that changes are necessary than to wait for them to be forced upon you. Responding to customer issues and opportunities, and putting their needs first, makes for a strong long-term relationship. Being proactive with a small issue stops it becoming a big issue. Implementing good ideas immediately for customers enhanced our reputation of being customer-focused.

Whether it is doing more of something that is great or taking action to stop things that are going wrong, you need to take immediate action. Sometimes this can be disruptive and cause short-term problems, but the sooner you make changes, the longer you will reap the benefits.

Action

Action

4   **Flexible**

Every business should have processes in place to give order and to ensure that everyone knows what the rules and parameters are to operate the business successfully. However, reality is that rules aren't always applicable to every situation. One rule doesn't always fit all.

Good management is about being flexible where you can be. It is good for business and it is good for the customer.

At JLA, we tried our utmost to deliver the machines to suit the customers' timings. There was no rigid delivery regime that was designed for economic savings.

If a customer needed a machine delivered on a Tuesday morning in Swindon, you would find other customers who were more flexible with their timing, so we would try to work everything out so that we had a flexible fit of deliveries around the more specific requirements, therefore satisfying everyone's needs.

For example, a washing machine is a vital part of the operation of a nursing home. If it was irreparable, they sometimes needed the machine the next day, which may not have been the usual delivery day for their area. We may have had to charge extra for that special delivery, but we would deliver and get the new machine up and running and keep the laundry operational.

Another example of flexibility was, that if personal circumstances made it difficult for staff to keep the standard hours, we were as flexible as possible with start times to accommodate them.

Flexible

Flexible

5   Passion

Passion, as we say throughout the book, comes from the top. If people didn't have passion for the job they were doing, they were in the wrong job and probably wouldn't last.

Passion to get things right for the staff, for the customer and also for our loyal suppliers. Passion means having fun and enjoying your life, and translates into success in business.

Passion

Passion

REUNEST 2016

Some vital actions to put into place before opening the doors.

How to borrow money

6   **How to borrow money**

In the early days, we were always quite successful at borrowing the money we needed to grow the business – thanks to my five years' working in a bank, and later, with Stuart's corporate finance background.

There are two parties to borrowing money - the borrower and the lender - and they don't always want the same thing. So the first thing is to make sure that whatever agreement you end up with, you are totally comfortable with the outcome.

Prepare a business plan and a budget that you believe in, and have assumptions that are realistic. Don't oversell.

Security may include a personal guarantee. You should only give a personal guarantee if you are comfortable doing it, and ring-fence the amount to the extent that your proposal requires. Once given, a personal guarantee is difficult to remove.

Always keep the lender informed – good news or bad. If you think you are going to breach the covenants of a loan, always be the one to tell the lender. Better to have them involved than to hope that the problem is going to go away.

Don't just back one horse. Approach more than one lender.

How to borrow money

Always have a Plan B

7   Always have a Plan B

People start a business with a Plan A. If they don't have a Plan B, they don't have a plan. Before you start, brainstorm the plan so that you have a good understanding of what your options are.

Know what could be business-critical and make sure that you are able to run with more than one horse. People you recruit may let you down. Your product may not arrive on time. You may have unforeseen issues. Floods, fires, some sort of accident.

If you have an alternative in your Plan B, or even a Plan C, you will start your business in a much stronger position. As you grow your business, continue to assess the risks and, if necessary, revise your Plan B to keep your options open.

Always have a Plan B

8 Data is your lifeblood

Start a business, buy a business. One of the first things to sort is the data. Who are your customers? What do they buy? What margins do you get? Who are your prospective customers? What is their potential? Who are your suspects?

When I started the business, the data was just scraps of paper, orders and my memory. JLA eventually developed a card system which told us when to make calls to customers, some details of their business and the equipment they had. After many trials and tribulations, we got to 'Goldmine', and data became the lifeblood of the business. We were able to identify customers who, for instance, only had a washer and no dryer. In one great flash of inspiration, we came up with an incentivised questionnaire programme, sending out 23,000 questionnaires to every nursing home in the country with a reward of a £5 M&S voucher for any questionnaire returned. The response was unbelievable. We were inundated, receiving more than 5,000 completed questionnaires. It didn't bring instant business but allowed us to build a database that kept rewards coming for years and years.

Data is the lifeblood of a business. Having great data is the basis of great decisions. So what is great data? Great data is relevant, it is clean and it is current.

Data is your lifeblood

9   Importance of contractual income

When we sold the business, the value we achieved was 90% from our contractual income.

Total care
The supply of the machine, installation and free service for the life of the contract. Usually over an eight-year period for a monthly fee.

Route
Usually to universities where again the machine was delivered, installed, and the laundry room decorated. The students paid to use the equipment, and instead of us getting a fee, we agreed a share of income with the university. Today, this is changing from students paying with cash in the machine to card operation for a similar shared income.

Included
The supply of a fully-maintained laundry at a fixed amount per month per resident. Sites were usually sheltered housing associations, universities and nurses' accommodation. This cost was added onto the normal rent and paid to the landlord who in turn paid us. Hence it was called 'Included'.

The value of a contract was generally four times the value of an outright sale. It gave us long-term income and, providing that we were delivering great service, we had a customer for life. Not only renewing the existing machines but as the organisations grew, supplying them with more equipment over the years.

Importance of contractual income

Spread the risk

10   Spread the risk

Being in business is risky, which is why the rewards for success are greater than those of risk-free investments.

Being reliant on limited sources of supply, or too few customers, takes control out of your hands. Your success becomes reliant upon their success.

I would say make sure you are not over-reliant on one customer.

JLA had a choice of suppliers and therefore was less exposed to supply-risk, and also had many customers. In addition, it had the benefit of long-term agreements with low-risk customers. These long-term agreements gave visibility of income into the future which would allow us time to change our business model if we were at risk.

Our biggest customer, Unite, represented 2% of our overall business. We would have hated to lose them, but if we had, we would still have 98% left.

Look at all the businesses that supplied just one major customer such as M&S or Poundland. Look at your business. Does one customer represent 20% of your customer base?

You need to grow other channels, other customers.

Spread the risk

11   Don't plan to fail, plan to succeed

Don't settle for second best. You are planning to succeed, not planning to fail. Hire the best, be in the best location, offer the best product and service – and shout it from the rooftops.

A man had a fruit and vegetable stall by the side of a main country road. He had adverts stuck on trees, promoting his great produce ahead. He stocked the best produce and opened seven days a week from 7am to 7pm. He was so successful that he sent his son to university to gain a business degree. When his son had learnt enough about business, he came home and started advising his father. "Take care Dad, there is a recession coming". When a few signs blew down, the son told his father not to replace them, to save money as there was a recession coming. The son was right. Business slowed down, and Mondays and Tuesdays were even slower. The son advised his father to save money on wages and electricity by closing on Mondays and Tuesdays. "Thank God my son is educated". Trade declined further and he saved on electricity by not illuminating the signs. The son was right, there was a recession, and his father ceased trading altogether.

When you start up your business, you must have a very positive outlook for the business you plan to run.

You mustn't have too many negative thoughts. As we have discussed, you need to be well-funded and not under-capitalised. This allows you to plan to succeed. You hire the best people and you open in the best location.

Since selling JLA, I have invested in a number of businesses. Three of the early ones failed. I invested in businesses with great ideas but which lacked good management, and had no plan to succeed. But I learnt lessons quickly. Now, we have several successful businesses in our style, and we are having fun.

Don't plan to fail, plan to succeed

Don't plan to fail, plan to succeed

Cash is king

12 Cash is king

More businesses fail due to poor cash flow than any other cause.

You need to do whatever is necessary to make sure that the cash flow is right. You can't bank stock, you can't bank debtors, you can't bank property.

Make sure that you have a long-term line of finance. Get everything in place, but if things suddenly have a downturn, turn your assets into cash even at a loss, but without damaging your long-term business.

Cash is king

13 First get your turnover then your profit

Get customers into the habit of buying from you, and then improve your profit margins to become profitable.

When a new business is opened or a new product brought to market, and particularly if it is a repeat purchase product, it is important in the initial stages to get customers to buy from you and to stop buying from their existing source. Often buyers are complacent and won't change unless you give them a reason to do so. As well as marketing and promotion, one reason to get them to change to you would be to promote the product or service on a below-cost price offer. This gets the customer to try you and your product or service. This generates new business opportunities, but not necessarily immediate profit.

Once the customer is in the habit of buying from you, you can move from the initial low price offer to a more commercial charge that gives you profit. You may lose some customers but you should also keep the majority of the new customers if done properly.

In 1973, Sue and I visited the Clean exhibition in Las Vegas. We were possibly the only English visitors there. Everyone wanted to talk to us and ask why we were there. We had recently bought a very run-down launderette in Withington, Manchester, and had invested quite a bit of money installing new machines, changing the décor and new signage outside, but still the shop was badly under-performing.

We went to the Wascomat stand and met a salesman, Charlie Gelfand. We got into conversation about how to promote a launderette. Charlie said that it is all about habit. Charlie asked me what side of the bed I slept on every night. Then he asked, when getting dressed in the morning, which leg did I put in my trousers first? You actually do it without thinking. Charlie said to put the price down to 10 pence per wash and then promote,

promote, promote. On our return to Manchester, we put Charlie's plan into action. Turnover went up and up and up. We ran the promotion until turnover levelled. We had nearly 1,000 new customers. We then put the price up to its normal £1 per wash. We had our turnover. Now we also had our profit.

The shop averaged over £2,500 per week for years and years.

First get your turnover then your profit

14   One office, preferably glass

Probably the most important factor in recruiting and keeping great staff is having a culture that they enjoy, in which they fit and in which they are allowed to flourish. Maintaining and protecting that culture is fundamental, but with multiple sites, this can be very difficult to sustain. Consistency of attitudes, management styles and standards can soon change if the business operates over a number of locations. Even separate buildings on one site can cause problems if there is limited interaction between staff. One office with communal respite areas, recreation rooms and dining facilities creates a feeling of oneness.

Glass offices with open-plan workspaces allow your eyes and ears to help monitor the morale and demeanour of the team. 'Not out of sight, out of mind'.

The major advantage of this was being able to read the team's body language. One of our great sales stars, Francis Ayscough, would always be in a spin — either buzzing on a high, or floundering in a low. Just by watching him walk into the office, I could tell which way things were going for him. The trick was to catch him just as he came off the high. Pick him up before he sank. Find out the problem, recharge his batteries, and send him back into the field selling for all he was worth.

One office, preferably glass

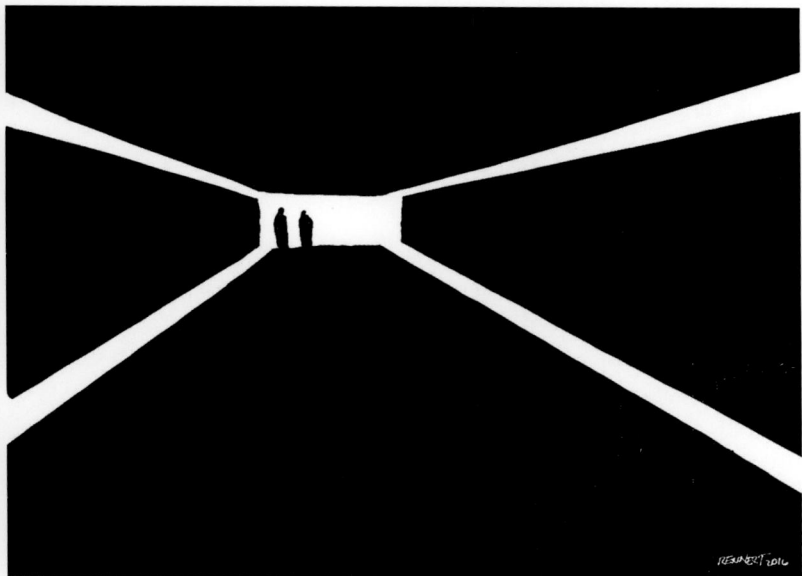

One office, preferably glass

15   Only deal with people you like

Life is too short to deal with people you don't like, don't trust or don't respect. There are plenty of business opportunities where a long-term relationship can be built through mutual respect. Enjoy your work with people you like.

We can't say we followed this to the letter. Although we loved our customers, there were some, over time, we would have preferred not to deal with. If that was the case, we didn't chase the business but accepted it if it came to us.

Regarding suppliers, we never had any formal distribution contracts as we dealt with people we trusted who, providing that we produced numbers, would honour our exclusivity. Many of the distributors became very close and personal friends of Sue and myself.

The whole process of buying machines was built on personal relationships and trust between our suppliers and us. One of our last relationships was with a large company in Asia which changed personnel almost annually, so we never really built a close or personal relationship with them. They proved to be the worst supplier we had ever dealt with. Our suppliers as manufacturers and us as distributors viewed the relationship to be a partnership.

People you like usually like you, they appreciate your exceptional service, and they pay you on time. If you make a mistake, they forgive you for it. They see that you are trying your best and respect you for it.

Only deal with people you like

16 Have budgets and targets

Budgets are for the business as a whole and targets are for individuals.

Budgets should be mainly written for the bank. If you write a budget that is achievable, and you hit that goal, the bank will be happy. Targets are written to drive the business forward. You must challenge your sales people. Challenge your marketeers. All targets must be achievable yet challenging. Build in a contingency, as certain things will go wrong during the year. We always hit our budgets and usually didn't achieve the full target. This still resulted in an average of over 20% growth for every year. The company was highly-driven.

Have budgets and targets

17   Your word is your bond

Reputation, respect, trust, the ability to sleep at night, are all under your own control, no-one else's. You have to earn these. You don't have to be liked, but in all walks of life, if your word is your bond, you will be respected.

Our reputation with suppliers was unique. We were always their best customers, not necessarily in the number of machines purchased (although frequently that was the case) but also, whether we promised to pay in 30, 60 or 90 days, we always paid on time.

When we gave a commitment to do something, we always made sure we delivered what we promised.

Your word is your bond

Your word is your bond

18 **Take 15 minutes**

Allocate time at the end of the day to look at what you have achieved, what has failed, what you will change and do differently tomorrow and review priorities. This is a great way to ensure the right thing is being done at the right time by the right people.

Update your priorities for the next day to avoid wasting t me on the wrong tasks that aren't in line with overall objectives. Put the urgent ones at the top of the page, don't carry fcrward ones that had a deadline that may have been missed and has become irrelevant, just cross them off.

A glance at your revised plan the following day when you are refreshed makes it easier to kickstart the day and, if necessary, make minor adjustments.

If you take these 15 minutes, you can leave the office and relax in the knowledge that you're all set up for the next day.

Take 15 minutes

19   Run your business as though you're never going to sell it

Run your business as though you're never going to sell it. When most people start a business, the main reason is to run a successful business without thought of selling it in the future.

As a business goes through different stages of development there will be different priorities. As a start-up business, getting customers and financial liquidity is more important than profit.

Once established, profitability, market share and growing the management become more important.

Make the right decision for the business in the present and you will have a great business going forward. If you make decisions because you think they are going to help you when you sell it, you will only succeed in harming the business.

However, when it comes to the time you have decided you are going to get out of the business and sell it, change your strategy and make decisions that build value for the sale and get better terms for your employees.

Run your business as though you're never going to sell it

20   One page/glanceable

I always insisted that any report had to be clear, concise and contained on one page. I think I even invented a word, that it had to be "glanceable". My feelings are so strong that if it was on more than one page it would be returned unread.

One page with bold headings, bullet points for each message to be conveyed, and containing only relevant information, is a great start.

Today at In Touch Networks, Matt insists his team present him with a SOAP - 'summary on a page', and this has helped the senior management team with their communication. The senior team needs to understand the bigger picture rather than getting bogged down in the detail and a one-page overview forces them to do this.

One page/glanceable

Glanceable

- Key items should be at the top of the schedule so even if they aren't all immediately actioned the most important ones get priority

- If sending via e-mail, make sure the person responsible for ownership is the direct recipient

- Other recipients that need to be aware of the message should only be cc'd

- You and other managers should be able to glance at the page, understand the message clearly and succinctly and take action

Glanceable

21 **Think big**

Once you have started your business and have sufficient sources of finance and working capital so as not to overtrade, then it is the time to THINK BIG.

Don't do things half-heartedly. If you are showing at an exhibition do it to make an impression and grab everyone's attention. If you are recruiting, recruit the best there is not just someone to fill a role to a budget.

In the early 90s we were compiling a mission statement about JLA, which included superlatives about quality of service and products supplied. By thinking big we eventually agreed to include a statement that,

"WE WANT TO BE FEARED BY THE COMPETITION"

That was thinking big and we achieved it.

If I hadn't decided to think big, JLA would have just been another small business.

Think big

Think big

REINHART 2016

22   A sense of urgency

Week to week, day to day, or hour by hour.

The sooner you know about a problem or an opportunity, the quicker you can deal with it.

If you have a reporting regime that works on a monthly cycle you aren't dealing with the here and now, but are dealing with history. What you want to do is change the future for the better. The more real-time your information and the greater the frequency of checking whether important targets are being met, the greater the sense of urgency. Check critical things in real-time, hourly and daily. This enables you to instantly identify any downturn in any area of the business. Running it this way affects staff behaviour and work levels, it produces a sense of urgency and allows you to find an immediate solution to any issue on the same day.

Most businesses used to run their financial reporting on a monthly basis. The problem with monthly figures is that by the time they're produced, they're at least four to six weeks out of date. How can you react to a blip in results that happened three weeks ago? How can you track what caused it? Your team is unlikely to remember what caused a drop in sales that long ago.

At JLA we always ran our business on a weekly or even daily basis.

If you leave any part of the business for a month there becomes a natural culture of "it's okay to have an off week" and the longer you leave a problem or a training need, the worse and more serious it becomes.

Today with In Touch Networks we track things in real-time and have golden numbers which are tracked hour by hour. These numbers are a specific and tailor-made set of KPIs that are crucial for monitoring the success of all areas of the business. For example, our staff incentive scheme, which is fully integrated with our CRM system, challenges employees to earn bonus on a daily basis. However, in order to access this bonus they must achieve weekly targets. They're driven daily and weekly, and it creates real urgency.

A sense of urgency

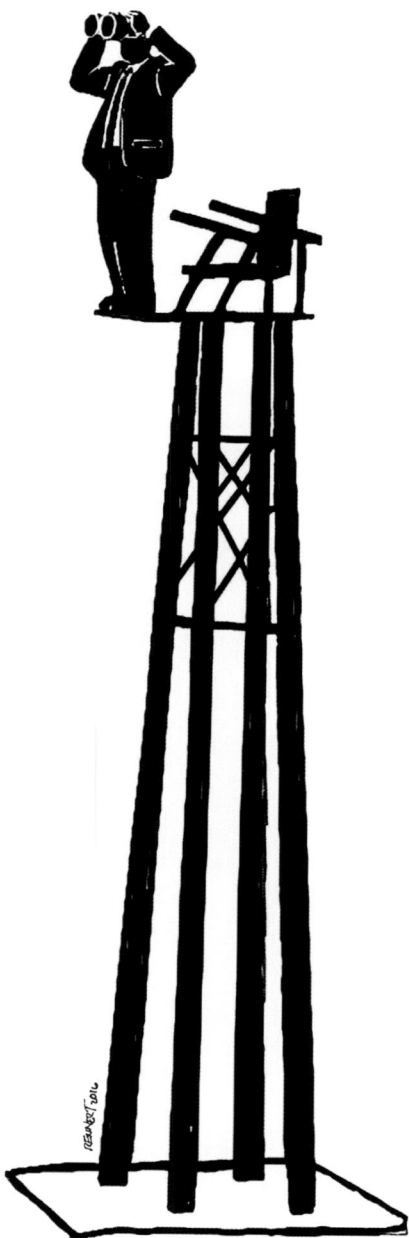

LOOKING FOR STAFF

Your staff are your most important asset. The more remote your premises are, the more difficult it is to find the right staff. Use every method you can think of. Reward staff for recommendations. Find people in bars, shops, the local community, even salesmen who visit you.

23. Build a team

24. Your first recruit should be your replacement

25. Recruit outside your industry

26. Hire less, pay more

27. Hire people with passion

28. Walk to work

29. You can't teach memory

30. IQ and EQ

Build a team

23   Build a team

Look at what you enjoy doing and that will be what you're good at.

Look at the gaps. My gaps were technical and no interest in too much intricate detail. Also, I had no experience of sales. I was good at buying and marketing - again no training but it just came naturally - and along with Sue, recruitment and reading people. So over time, the first two recruits were technical, then a financial controller. Stuart and I headed up the business. Stuart was brilliant at running the day-to-day and the detail of the business. My areas of expertise were new ideas, motivation, relationships with suppliers, marketing, and knowing what the market needed, when. By then, Sue was Head of HR to ensure that JLA built a team that fitted our culture. Richard Logan was our superb, realistic Finance Director. Dick Cardis had developed from Sales into a brilliant Marketing Director. John Swailes was our gung-ho Sales Director, and Ted Hirst looked after Technical Sales. We were backed up by many great people who had grown with the business having been there since they were in their teens.

You never stop building a team, but it may take 20 years to get the right team.

Build a team

24 Your first recruit should be your replacement

I say this even though it took me 17 years to find my replacement. From the early days, I recruited people to take over positions in which I was weak. First, a Finance Director then an Operations Director and finally, 17 years on, I met Stuart and knew that he was my replacement as CEO. Stuart and I worked as a team for over 20 years playing to each other's strengths. As I used to say, Stuart did all the boring bits.

By recruiting your replacement, you strengthen the business and allow yourself space to grow. Running a business is not the same as growing a business.

Your first recruit should be your replacement

25   Recruit outside your industry

When we looked for new sales staff, we occasionally recruited from within the laundry industry. In most cases, this was a mistake. They had been taught to sell laundry machines, not solutions.

We found that it was harder to retrain someone who had a pre-conceived idea of how they should sell in our markets because they had come from a competitor that sold rather than rented. The cultures of our competitors were also different from ours. They weren't customer-focused as often they were from manufacturers who are more product and technically-focused.

Our biggest success came from looking elsewhere. People who didn't sell features, they sold benefits. We recruited from the photocopier world, a bus salesman, even a sandwich salesman and a fork-lift truck salesman. These people knew how to solve customers' problems. This is why our sales people achieved an average of at least double that of our competitors.

Recruit outside your industry

26   Hire less, pay more

Recruit quality people, not just numbers. Don't be too rigid with pay guidelines. Always be somewhat flexible for the star candidate. This will make life much easier. The job is what the person doing the job makes of it, and therefore it is the person you should be valuing, not the job.

Hire less, pay more

Hire less, pay more

27 Hire people with passion

The passion comes from the top. At the top of JLA, we had great people with great passion. John Swailes, Dick Cardis, Richard Logan, Clive Hadfield, Dave Wheatcroft, Malcolm Brook and hundreds of others.

If ever a man epitomises passion, it is Dave Wheatcroft.

Dave joined JLA over 30 years ago on a Youth Training Scheme. At 16, he started in accounts. Not the greatest accountant - but you could already see his passion. He quickly moved through many departments; distribution, service and, by the age of 20, internal sales.

He successfully made appointments, sold machines on the telephone then moved into field sales in the launderette market. He moved to London.

A Service Manager role came up - he applied and eventually he became National Service Manager.

He had no formal training and no university degree, but his passion carried him through.

When I sold, he continued at JLA in the new corporate structure and found it hard to adapt, and his passion waned.

In 2014, we had a chat and he is now successfully working as Sales Director at In Touch Networks – one of our businesses.

The passion is back.

Passion brings drive, energy, enthusiasm and a will to win. You either have passion or you don't.

Hire people with passion

Hire people with passion

28   Walk to work

We were in a location in the small village of Ripponden with a population of about 6,000 people. It was not the greatest location to attract top-quality staff. So we had an incentive scheme of £200 for any recommendation from existing staff that turned into a recruit.

Despite the location, we didn't lose many good employees We then had a brilliant idea of producing thousands of copies of a four-page newsletter with the headline 'Walk to work' and had it delivered within a three-mile radius, trying to encourage people to work local instead of commuting into Manchester or Leeds

The newsletter invited people to attend an open day one Saturday morning. We had about 30 employees in the office to create the usual buzz, ten people conducting interviews and creating shortlists and a psychometric analyst to create instant profiles. We did this four or five times, during which we attracted over 200 people and employed around 15 of those. It was a great success!

We compared the experience of working in the nearby towns and cities and realised that as well as working for a great company, there were other major benefits to the employee, such as:

- Fast growing company
- Opportunities for promotion
- Short travel time on foot, by car or public transport
- Free parking
- On-site staff restaurant
- Free racquetball court
- Free gym
- Free children's pantomime at Christmas
- Subsidised sports and social activities
- Free bonfire and fireworks display
- Subsidised laundry

JLA was a great place to work.

Walk to work

29 You can't teach memory

You can't teach memory. If someone has a bad memory, look for signs during the interview. If they have a poor memory, they must have a foolproof system to back up that poor memory, without either of these they are virtually unemployable. Without a good memory, they won't hold information at the forefront of their minds while assimilating an argument. This leads to a lack of clarity and judgement, and poor negotiation skills.

The rule is if it's a poor memory then they need a good system.

You can't teach memory

Everyone knows the meaning of the measurement of IQ. In the early 1990s, psychometric profiling became a huge part n our recruitment of the right staff. The questionnaires allowed us an insight into IQ levels and a little about the EQ (Emotional Quotient or Emotional Intelligence) of candidates. The results of these profiles representec about 20% of our decision process on whether to employ somebody and whether they would fit into the culture of the business. Studies have shown that people with a higher EQ have greater mental health, exemplary job performance and more potent leadership skills.

As we found out to our cost over a number of years, managers who joined us from the corporate world usually could not fit into our fast-moving, flexible flat management structure.

Psychometric profiling is not a perfect science. If the results indicated that a particular person was right for the job, and we employed them, in reality this wasn't necessarily true. The individual might turn out to be right or might turn out to be wrong. On the other hand, if the results indicated that it was the wrong candidate, and we still employed them, then in 100% of these cases, the appointment turned out to be wrong. The original psychometric assessment was always right.

We became such a believer in profiling that we would even profile people who were on temporary assignments, just to make sure that they fitted in. We had a great profiler in A an Glover of Elenchus Approach Ltd, who helped us to use and interpret the results.

IQ and EQ

IQ and EQ

KEEPING STAFF

When you have good or great staff, don't lose them. Keep them interested and motivated, and make sure they feel members of the team.

31. The bus is in town

32. Train, train, train

33. You can't fit the person to the job, so fit the job to the person

34. Be good at hiring, great at firing

35. Reward spectacular failure

36. Condemn mediocre success

37. S.T.O.P.

38. Find and fire terrorists

39. Work hard, play hard

40. Teamwork

41. Bottom 10%

The bus is in town

31 The bus is in town

Grab opportunities straight away and don't procrastinate.

Many people describe their success partially by being in the right place at the right time. Mostly, this isn't true. It's more about having the insight to grab an opportunity when you recognise the potential, and taking it.

There are virtually no business opportunities that do not have some element of risk, and usually it is the element of risk that causes people not to take up an opportunity. Another way of describing this is the cliché 'He who dares, wins'.

There are countless examples where an opportunity was missed because the potential wasn't seen or the risk deemed too great.

Francis Ayscough was a JLA star. He had joined the Royal Horse Guards at 15 (not quite telling the truth about his age). He served 12 years, and during his illustrious career, he even got blown off a roof by an IRA bomb.

He then looked for a career on Civvy Street but he was very unsure of his direction. He joined JLA as Service Manager. We could see that he had talent, but probably not in management.

Over a five-year period, he left and rejoined three times. Finally, he left for a fourth time. I offered him a great role. I said, "The bus is in town". He considered it, but the bus left.

After five years in the wilderness, he rang me. I said, "I have another bus in town, and don't miss this one".

Grab the opportunity today as tomorrow it might not be there.

The bus is in town

32 Train, train, train

You recruit great people. They are experienced and know what they are doing. But having a continuous training programme is vital to the success of any business. For example, salesmen had targets to sell and rent machines, although rental was viewed as the more important target to achieve. A salesman, who in four consecutive weeks didn't achieve his rental target, would spend two or three hours every Friday with Stuart being trained and re-trained in how to sell rental.

Training is one of the biggest motivators in any business. Whether it is knowledge, practical skills or technique that is being developed, the outcome is always positive.

When business is tough, one of the first budgets often cut is the training budget. In our case, we would always invest in our people to make sure that we were equipping them to the best level possible to deal with difficult times.

Training would be carried out by a combination of in-house people and external specialists.

Internal training was little and often to re-focus on existing skills and techniques or promote new techniques or product knowledge.

Some members of management had a rather short-sighted attitude to training as they were viewing things in the short term. A short-term drop in performance as a result of being off the road (for training) was soon over-compensated for in the long term by the increased skill set or knowledge due to the training.

When we introduced OTEX, which was our revolutionary laundry process that killed all superbugs, it was a different sell. As with all training we did, it was about the customer's business and what OTEX would do for the customer. It required a change in approach. All of the salesmen were brought into the office on a Monday to receive training, and they continued to be trained every Monday until they finally started to rent OTEX consistently.

Train, train, train

33 **You can't fit the person to the job, so fit the job to the person**

In practice, it is extremely rare to find a person whose range of skills, expertise and personality are a perfect fit to the job description. Even if they do, very often the role evolves over time, so some skill sets or experiences are more relevant than others. However, the employee's skills may not develop n the direction or to the extent that the role requires. Recognise this, as without this match, the quality of the work and the job satisfaction will suffer, and subsequently the business will suffer. It may even result in a really good employee wanting to leave the business as the job is unsuitable.

Review the skills and ability of the employee, and if they substantially match the job requirements, but not totally, take those elements that do not work and have them carried out by someone else who is capable of doing them. Fit the job to the person, not the person to the job.

Recruitment is a very expensive process. Sometimes however, you find a great person but you give them the wrong job. Search the organisation to see if there is a role that better fits the person.

Dick Cardis, who eventually was our superb Marketing Director, started as a mediocre salesman but was highly intelligent and always had great ideas. We successfully moved him from sales to marketing and he was one of our greatest successes.

Louise Webster started as a very disorganised office Sales Manager and was completely failing in her role. We talked. She rather liked the idea of field sales and became our top Key Account Sales Manager.

These types of role-changes happened hundreds of times throughout the business, giving us a loyal, happy, hard-working and successful team.

You can't fit the person to the job, so fit the job to the person

34   Be good at hiring, great at firing

When Sue started the recruitment process, we were good. For management and sales, we had formal interviews, usually with Stuart and Sue, followed by a more relaxed interview with me. It was important to find out if they were capable of doing the job we needed. It was more important to feel that they would fit into our culture.

At JLA, it became the norm that if people lasted the first few months, they stayed for years and years. If we thought that a new recruit wasn't coming up to the standard we expected, we had a quiet word. We tried training. If no improvement, we had to become great at firing.

If the person isn't right, don't prolong the agony. It's better for all if they move on.

It is not possible to get it right all of the time and, inevitably, if you get it wrong, you need to respond to the failing. You can assess whether additional training will make the difference, or put them in another role in which they might excel. If you can't find a solution then you need to fire them but treat them fairly and offer help.

Do what is right for the business and then show them some compassion for their circumstances.

We had a long-serving sales person who had lost his passion for the business and was no longer successful. Success or failure is the easiest thing to measure in a salesman because it usually equates to the value of the business won in any week.

There is a long, drawn-out process required under employment legislation to terminate long-term employment that can often take months to conclude, when both parties will often know what the inevitable outcome will be.

To follow the procedure would have resulted in the salesman going through weeks of anguish knowing that his heart wasn't in it, and the business and customers would suffer because they weren't getting the attention they deserved.

We sat down with the salesman and confirmed his unhappiness in the role, agreeing that he needed to leave the business and move on. He said he hadn't resigned because he hadn't yet found alternative employment, but he was unhappy in his work. We agreed a termination settlement which was greater than he was likely to get if we had followed the employment regulations. This allowed him to move on and so we could openly recruit his replacement.

A strong business doesn't carry passengers.

Be good at hiring, great at firing

35   Reward spectacular failure

Targets can either be brilliantly motivating or dangerously demoralising. Targets should be challenging but achievable. Without both of the components, they do not work for either the company or the employee. To keep growing a company, targets should ensure that the business and its people are always challenged and rewarded. The more successful the employee - the more successful the company.

Spectacular failure. We gave Lara Wade, a Key Account Sales Manager, a new target. In fact, we doubled her figures from £1million to £2million. We predicted that her marketplace was going to boom and we promised to appoint another telesales person and a junior Field Sales Manager. During the year, we failed to find the right recruits. By the end of the year, Lara had achieved a 57% growth, obviously much less than target. Her manager was unhappy with her performance. By this time, Stuart and I had left the business. Unfortunately, the new management considered her to have failed, and she also left the business. If Stuart and I had still been there in charge, she would have been a hero and we would have rewarded her spectacular failure.

Reward spectacular failure

John Greenwood was a good salesman but not too driven. He had a comfort level and would, each year, achieve his target probably by less than 1%. We didn't actually condemn it but decided that we could achieve much more out of his area. He had a telesales girl working with him, June McLean. June was just part-time and would only become full-time if she had a job in the field. We divided the area into two, giving John the choice of East or West. John chose West which was the better area. June took East. John maintained his 101% of target and within six months, June was out-selling him by more than 20%. So in a way, we condemned the mediocre success.

Condemn mediocre success

37 **S.T.O.P.**

Striving **To**wards **P**erfection

Canvas your people for their opinion. Managers aren't the only people who can come up with great ideas. Anyone who has a passion for what they do, and has an opinion, is worth asking.

When wanting to stay ten steps ahead of the competition, we produced a three-page document entitled 'S.T.O.P.' and gave a copy to each employee. We gave them a £10 incentive to complete and return it.

Page 1 asked them to tell us how we could improve their work environment.

Page 2 asked them to tell us how they could improve their work experience and efficiency.

Page 3 asked them to tell us how we could improve our customers' experience or our business offering.

Almost all of our employees completed it. We paid £100 for any idea we implemented. We paid £1,000 for the best idea. The £1,000 award went to a Service Engineer. At the time, we were building our reputation for the best service for our Total Care customers, and so we had introduced a guaranteed service response time of eight working hours. If we were a day late, we gave the customer a week's rent back, two days – two weeks' rent and, if over three days late, a full month.

The Engineer said that the original idea was great but that it was a complicated message to market. Why not just say that if we take more than eight hours to respond, we give £100 to the customer. This was a massively-improved message and set the standard for the industry.

S.T.O.P.

38　**Find and fire terrorists**

No matter how good your recruitment process is, occasionally a terrorist will get through.

Terrorists make it their life's ambition to exaggerate the negative and make a virtue of complaining. The damage they can do to lower morale and positivity is immense and they should be removed from the business at any cost. The long-term damage caused by them remaining in the business will have far greater consequences than removing them.

A very nice person worked in the office, but they could moan, complain and depress your most passionate people. At first, we thought they were in the wrong role so we moved them. They complained about everything. We tried talking and counselling, but in the end we fired them.

We preferred to pay wrongful dismissal costs than to suffer the depression that she caused to her colleagues and team.

Find and fire terrorists

39   Work hard, play hard

We had fantastic, loyal people. We had a long-service board with people who had been with us for 10, 20 or even over 30 years. That didn't mean that everyone who joined stayed – a lot of people found the work too hard. In fact, we made an acquisition, in Scotland, where unfortunately or maybe fortunately, our reputation for hard work preceded us and, after the owner of business announced and introduced JLA as the new owners, within days, 60% of the staff walked out. This gave us a short-term problem but in the long term, we had made a success that went from strength to strength.

We also played hard. Any excuse for a party or celebration. At one successful open day, I set a high target of sales to be achieved in a day. If they were successful, I agreed to take a dip in the river on 1 May! I staggered out of the river soaked to the skin and freezing cold. I didn't realise how cold the river would be but they more than smashed the target and I got a little wet, to the cheers of one hundred people, customers included.

Work hard, play hard

Work hard, play hard

40 Teamwork

Look at the illustration, two people working together. If one lets go, that's the end for both. It fantastically illustrates the need to work together in business.

In every department, and with other departments, you need to work at it. As JLA grew teams became more diverse and drifted apart. We organised a monthly event hosted by a different department each time. We gave them a budget to provide food and soft drinks, and they had to find an entertaining way of showing the rest of the company what they did, the issues and successes they were having. Sometimes it was just fact on display, sometimes comic and once we were shown a 30-minute play of a typical day in Marketing.

Teamwork is key to future success.

Teamwork

Teamwork

41 **Bottom 10%**

Every 6 months, have each manager draw up a league table of their staff. The best at the top, the worst at the bottom. If the same people are in the bottom two places for more than two quarters, question their suitability. Re-train, counsel, change their role or if all else fails, decide they are in the wrong job or the wrong company.

Bottom 10%

Bottom 10%

V MOTIVATING YOUR PEOPLE

Teamwork is key. When you find your team doing something right, let them know. Work hard with your team and play hard with your team.

Look after your staff

Your staff are your most valued asset. If you recruit well, and ensure that they have the same attitude and work ethic as your business culture, then they should stay and grow with the business.

Invest in them with training and education, and share your business success with them as if they are part-owners.

Be interested in their family, as family will be the most important thing to them.

Pay them what they are worth to the business, not what you can get away with.

Assess them regularly and tell them how they are progressing, and take appropriate action.

Provide them with a great working environment.

Look after your staff

43   **We believe in incentives**

In the early days, we incentivised sales staff, field staff and nternal sales staff. Did it work? Yes! The downside was that the rest of the company was envious, so we widened it to the whole company.

What incentives did we run?

- New York on Concorde, back on the QE2
- LA Olympics 1984 – ticket for the finals
- private plane to Venice for lunch for the eight top sales people
- overnight to Iceland for a game of midnight golf
- private plane to Rome for sight-seeing and shopping
- Team Bologna
- telesales trip by limousine to London
- weekly dinner for two

The best incentive of all was "THE BRIEFCASE". I was in a meeting room with the whole of the sales team. There was a knock on the door and in walked a security guard with a briefcase handcuffed to his wrist. He handed the briefcase to me and fastened the handcuff to my right wrist. He then walked to the door and stood guard.

I walked to the centre of the U-shaped table around which the sales staff were seated and standing, and announced that the competition had only one winner. I opened the case and inside was £20,000 in cash. Walking around the room, I showed the salesmen the money, some touched it. They had never seen £20,000 in cash! Whoever achieved the top target sales over the next 13 weeks took the lot - tax paid. The whole £20,000. As a result, sales overall were up by £300,000. So the economics really worked. The winner was the number three salesman who said he needed it to buy a new home. More importantly, he had always been a £20,000 a week man but now proved he could sell £30,000 a week. The winner, Jeremy Ball, won by a few hundred pounds more than Martin Aston, who was slightly annoyed, but he too, as a result of the incentive, had achieved record sales.

We believe in incentives

44   Pull not push

Motivating people is always easier, and more successful, when they are in tune with you and see what you want them to do as a shared idea. Then you can pull the team along with you in a decision, rather than pushing them into something they don't fully agree with.

Pushing people will usually result in low commitment. Asking the team their opinion and including them in the discussion, without telling them what decision you anticipate, allows you to modify the final decision to include any valid input that comes from the discussion. A team will fully believe in and get behind a decision they helped to shape.

Giving an instruction without consultation or explanation has never been motivational or the most successful way of achieving company objectives. Pushing takes a lot more management time than pulling. Always pull, never push.

Pull not push

45   Incentivise everybody

Inspiring and motivating staff - even the most passionate - is an integral part of getting the best out of them. What motivates one person may not motivate another, so we follow one of our other rules to get to extraordinary incentives for everyone, which is 'getting to WOW'.

An incentive should live up to its name and make anyone who has the opportunity to particpate, really want to win.

Although financial incentives are often very good because they allow the winner to buy that one thing that they really want, and that alone drives them cn to win, it is not the only thing. Providing a once-in-a-lifetime experience that will live with someone forever and be recounted over the years as one of the best experiences that person ever had, has proven to be an extraordinary incentive.

Incentivising teams of people of different disciplines within the business to achieve new levels of customer service together has proved to have a long-lasting effect on business, and raised the level of customer service going forward permanently.

Novel ideas to incentivise customers to buy or engage with you, and help you understard the needs that they have in a better way, should also be considered regularly because extraordinary incentives can often produce extraordinary results.

Everyone in a business is important and needs to be incentivised. One of the best incentives when someone is doing a great job is to tell them. Visualise it, put a league table up, e-mail them, put your arm around them, tell them how great they are and let the whole team know.

Incentivise everybody

46   Agendas and deadlines

An agenda should be all questions. Challenging questions. Then all the team present prioritise them, with actions, ownership and deadlines. Ban the words 'ongoing' or 'TBC' - you need a deadline date.

Agendas and deadlines

47   Top dog

Being recognised and celebrated by peers and colleagues as the very best in their field, and collecting an award for it, can often be better than a financial incentive.

We had a Top Dog competition with a leader board where the salesmen were ranked in order of percentage of target. At the end of each week, the ranking changed with some salesmen going up the ranking and others going down, depending on how good a week they had had.

Rivalry was intense as pride was at stake, and the figures were very close.

Although sales figures were normally very open and visible on the screens around the office and included in weekly reports, we decided for the last two weeks of the incentive not to publicise the figures, but just change the rankings. No-one knew how close they were to the next person on the board because the information was withheld.

The outcome was that over those last two weeks, the rivalry was so intense, and the closeness of the ranking unknown, that sales went through the roof to try to become Top Dog.

Success is often a greater motivator than money.

Top dog

Top dog

48 A winning culture

Any successful business needs to create a winning culture. Celebrate every win however small. Cheer, clap or reward every success. If it is a loss, quickly analyse why, make effective changes and move on.

Tell everybody about company successes, put statistics up on screens, shout about it on boards, charts, send e-mails, tell everybody how great the company is doing.

To succeed, you need to pull your team with you and create a winning culture. You set goals and targets and then persuade the team to go in the direction you want to go.

In sport, when a player or a team wins, adrenaline flows through the veins and gives them an addictive buzz. People become addicted to winning. This is why some football team managers can take certain players and transform them from losers to winners as they create a winning culture that everyone wants to be a part of.

Someone who was addicted to winning was our sales director, John Swailes. Our main market was nursing homes and small hotels and John would go door to door selling commercial laundry machines to B&Bs in Blackpool.

Most people would become despondent at having Blackpool's landladies slamming the door in their faces. But with each door slammed, John rejoiced with a celebratory fist pump. His explanation was that each 'no' brought him closer to a sale. This demonstrated John's resilience, ambition and pass on for winning. He was able to bring this back to the office and help us maintain our winning culture.

A winning culture

A winning culture

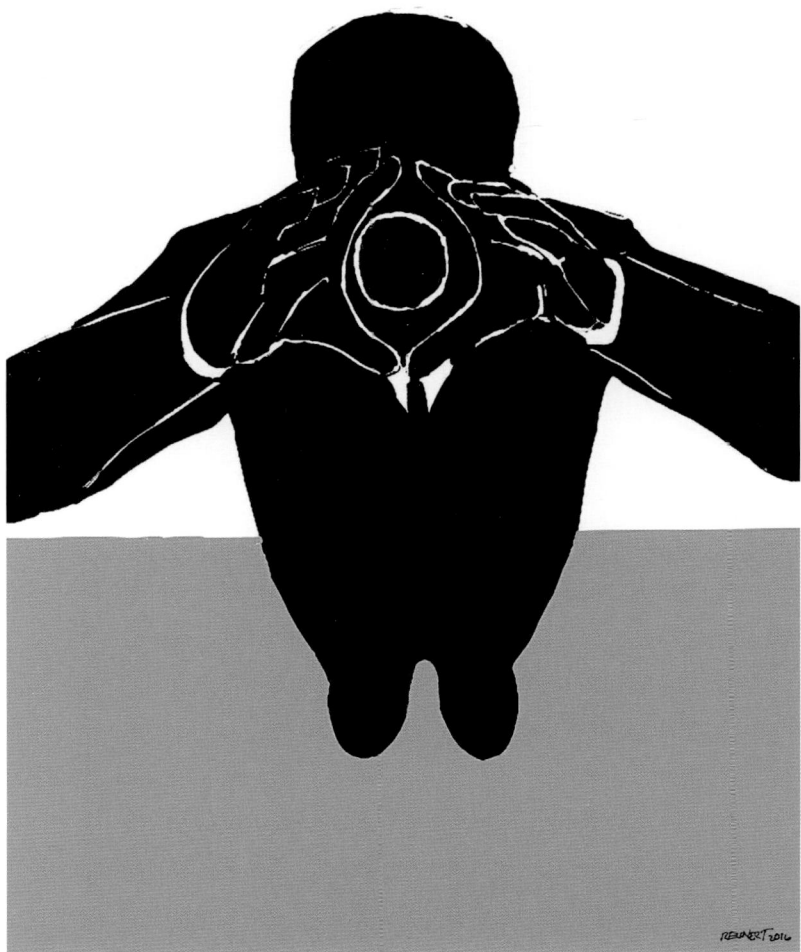
RENNERT 2016

vi GETTING YOUR MESSAGE TO MARKET

Your customers need to know how good you are. Shout it from the rooftops. Use everything you can to inform potential customers. Use telesales, mailshots, PR, marketing, search engine optimisation and social media.

Defend your brand to the death

49 Defend your brand to the death

Establishing a brand is the most effective way, over time, to publicise what your business stands for, and should be instantly recognisable. Branding does not happen overnight and may take years to get established.

Once you understand brand, you must defend it with everything you can. 'JLA' became a brand without a plan to make it such.

We created a brand without realising it, and after almost 30 years of using 'JLA' as our brand, we approached a specialist, respected brand business, The Attic. They conducted an exercise where they interviewed 50 members of our staff, our competitors, over 100 of our customers and all of our suppliers. The message was that we had the strongest and warmest brand they had ever worked with. From then on, brand became everything.

We had sub-brands, for instance 'Laundry FM', which was our rental business. Immediately, admin and accounts staff abbreviated it to 'LFM'. I put out a warning that anybody found using the abbreviated version would be dismissed on the grounds of gross misconduct. It may sound harsh but I was defending our brand to the death by insisting on only using 'Laundry FM'.

Defend your brand to the death

50 One message

When trying to get a customer's attention, have one message.
Whether it's an advert, a flyer, a poster or a web page.
Remember, white space sells. You may be selling a product, a
service or even recruiting. Don't confuse. Have total clarity.
One message works.

One message

51 **A.I.D.A.**

Since time immemorial, all marketing should follow this rule:

A   Attention   In a microsecond, you have to grab the customer's attention.

I   Interest   First, you grab their attention.
Now you have to spark their interest.

D   Desire   Make them want what you are selling.

A   Action   Give them a call to action.
A telephone number, e-mail address, an address to visit.

Adverts must include all of the above in the above order.

A.I.D.A.

Launderette owners were our first customers. As we matured, we became more sophisticated with our mailshots.

Electrolux were dumping machines in the UK launderette market at crazy prices.

I got on a plane and went to see Mike Bohe of IPSO, one of our major suppliers. I said that we couldn't compete and that we needed a better price.

Mike understood the situation. I ordered five times the number of machines at one time, ordering 1,000 machines with a 30% discount. We hit the market with a glossy, price-based mailshot and only gained a few sales. The mailshot paper was too thick and the whole effect too glossy, so the offer was not perceived as a bargain. We then photocopied the mailshot on thinner paper in black and white, and mailed again. Sales exploded. The thinner paper and the black and white print made the offer look like the bargain it was, and customers bought.

Make your message match your pitch

53 'Free' is the most powerful word in marketing

In marketing, there is no stronger word to use than 'free'.

Everyone likes a bargain, but even more so, everyone likes to get something free or extra to what they were originally looking to buy. The word 'free' grabs attention and makes the reader want to read on. In reality, nothing is free, but if an alternative supplier isn't giving you the same free offer, it looks like it is free.

We would offer free laundry surveys. This was a way to get in front of the customer and see their problems so that we could then suggest solutions and gain orders where previously there was no obvious demand.

We used to offer free rental for six months, and the customer would sign the contract which could be cancelled within six months. But we knew that once the machine was installed, they would love it so much that they would want to keep it. We would also offer:

- free service
- free towels to hairdressers
- free detergent to care homes
- free delivery
- free installation
- free training

The element that is being offered as free will often be the clincher that makes the customer buy from you.

'Free' is the most powerful word in marketing

54   Where there is mystery there is margin

Today, with price comparison sites and online shopping it is fairly easy to take away the mystery in some products, and this has driven prices and therefore inflation down.

However, where you can add mystery to your product, you can make good margin. The more things you can bundle together the better, such as delivery, installation, training, service As an example, we made a good margin on OTEX. We had spent more than £2million over a number of years developing a product which could kill all superbugs in the wash. The product saved money and was hygienically perfect, but there was a lot of mystery surrounding it. So we didn't overcharge but we could get a fair margin from the product and recover our development costs.

Where there is mystery there is margin

55 Remember what business you are in

Luckily, most of our competitors thought they were in the laundry business.

The biggest competitor was Electrolux. Why did we win and they fail? One simple reason: Electrolux had the best machines, the best range, and the best world brand, but they thought they were in the laundry business. Their salesmen had to understand the washing process in finite detail.

At JLA, we knew that the business we were in was the same business as our customers – we were in the care home business, the hotel business, the army, the prison business, the university business.

What really mattered was the great service. Yes, we had to have reliable, easy-to-operate machines, but when they broke down, we had to offer great service. We matched our machines and our product to meet our customers' needs.

Remember what business you are in

56   Getting to WOW

This point is to emphasise the importance of meeting and exceeding expectations. Whether it is to a customer, a supplier or even an employee, producing a response of WOW, being an expression of amazement, is the response you should be looking for.

What is being proposed here is that whatever you set out to achieve in a business relationship, you need to impress If you don't impress, you become forgettable and merge in with the also-rans.

You can get a WOW from:

- speed of response
- quality of presentation
- level of service

Almost anything that is better than what the competition offers, and what the customer expects, will contribute to WOW

Getting to WOW is about making the experience of buying and operating as painless and enjoyable as possible.

Users of equipment want reliability, and then good service when it breaks down – which it inevitably will. Customers don't expect a machine to run faultlessly forever, but it is their experience in having it repaired when it does break down that is likely to be remembered, and dictates the business relationship in the future.

In one instance, a care home customer with only one washing machine and dryer had a breakdown of their dryer. The engineer, Paul Emery, attended and tried his best to repair the machine but was lacking a part to get the machine fully operational. Another engineer in the adjacent area had the part, and arrangements were made to meet, get the part and return to repair the broken dryer.

Paul's next call was a launderette, and it was here that he would meet and get the part. To help the care home, he took the washed, but as yet undried, bed linen with him to the launderette, and as he repaired the broken machine at the launderette, he dried the linen. He then returned to the care home with the dried linen and the part, repaired the dryer and got a WOW from his customer.

Getting to WOW

57   Understand each type of customer and deal with them individually

Every customer is different, as each person is different. Good selling is about understanding your customer, their business, their business problems, and making your solution tailor-made for them. The more you can match your offering to their needs, the more business you will win. Being flexible helps you to remove some of the things they don't need and add in others that they do need.

Sometimes customers confuse what they might like with what they actually need. Therefore, understanding what would be "nice to have" if it was free, and what is a "must have", is part of the selling process. In doing this, the salesman must balance out the cost of components of the package with the benefits the customer gets from having them. It is not what the salesman sees as value, but what the customer sees as value.

Dealing with customers as individuals is not only about the offering that you propose, but how they are dealt with personally. If they are formal, mirror their formality. If they require a lot of detail, give them the detail. The more rapport you build, the more the customer will feel comfortable dealing with you. Deal with them how they want to be dealt with, not how you would want to be dealt with.

In business, you only continue to exist if you have customers. So whatever business your customers are in – that's the business you are in. Learn the language of your customer and they will talk to you and listen to you.

Care home managers talk about clients, residents, beds, incontinence, cost per week, horizontal evacuation, C.diff, thermal disinfection. Hoteliers talk about occupancy levels, rack rate, wet sales, par stock, back of house.

Training sales people is about training them to understand what is important to your customers, so recruit and train people to be hotel specialists, care specialists. Train them, not about what your product and company does, but what it does for the customer.

Understand each type of customer and deal with them individually

58   Generate leads from the field

We had engineers in the field attending over 3,000 jobs each week. In every call, they had the opportunity to see the customers' laundries and speak to the people who used them. They were the eyes and ears of the salesmen.

They were trusted by customers, because if it was economical to repair, the engineers would repair it. If, however, the machine was beyond economic repair, and the customer was told by the engineer that they would be throwing good money after bad, the customer would listen. The engineer would report the lead to the sales team, and the sales team would contact the customer.

We had one person in the office looking after all of the engineers' leads to ensure that they got paid commission when the machine was delivered, to encourage them to introduce more leads. We ran a league table showing how much the leads from engineers had generated in sales, which probably represented 25% of our overall sales.

Generate leads from the field

59 A photograph is worth a thousand words

Delivering a WOW service relies upon teamwork. Field staff visiting sites could be salesmen, Service Engineers, delivery drivers, trainers, trouble-shooters and installers. Getting it right first time is a big part of great service.

Office staff are often required to understand information sent in by field staff to provide a solution for customers. Pictures taken on a camera phone and sent to the office can immediately show the office-based staff what needs to be actioned to get a solution.

A photograph of a difficult access for delivery can show the delivery staff what equipment-handling may be required.

A photograph of inadequate utility services will pre-warn the installer what to expect and what he would need.

Even if the photograph does not fully explain the issue when both field and office staff are both able to see the same thing, it allows them to have a much more meaningful discussion.

We issued field staff with cameras to take photographs to attach to a customer's record, so that when we contacted the customer, we had an idea of the customer's premises and the state of their laundry room. This was far better than a written description.

Getting it right first time is better service and significantly less costly.

A photograph is worth a thousand words

Manufacturers understandably protect their know-how, and in today's market, their products are for a global market, with only minor changes from one region to another.

However, there may be instances where the product is not a perfect match and needs modification. Manufacturers are reluctant to make such changes when the volumes are relatively small, leaving the distributor to either accept the product with its limitations or make the changes themselves.

If it is possible to make these changes, this gives the distributor a massive commercial advantage.

In 2011, having sold JLA the previous year, I was contacted by Philippe Castaignos of Schneidereit in Germany who really wanted to meet me. Eventually I agreed to meet him in London, not expecting a very enlightening conversation. However, within the first twenty minutes, I was fascinated by Schneidereit's business model. Like JLA, they were in the laundry equipment business. However, they only rented machines, they didn't sell them. Every machine they imported, whether it was from Sweden, Spain or Korea, came to their workshops and was then aesthetically and technically modified, and left their premises as a German machine, all branded 'Schneidereit, Solingen'. A German machine for the German market but also branded strongly with colour. Each machine was programmed and labelled for specific markets: Mop, Easy Care, Beauty. In this way, over time, they had come to dominate each of their specific markets.

So, Schneidereit created a German machine because Germans prefer to buy German products. Instead of a washing machine, there was a specific machine designed for each of their different marketplaces. They made the machine, the market and the solution uniquely theirs.

They tested every machine in extreme conditions and replaced all vulnerable parts, so the machines became more reliable with fewer breakdowns and lower service costs.

We liked the idea so much that in 2012, we bought 75% of the business.

Schneidereit it

61 Good is good enough, perfect is too late

One prime example. Cherie Laney, a daughter of a great friend of ours, had a marketing degree from the University of California but she was finding it hard to find a position without any work experience. Her father asked me to do her a favour. Could she come over and work in the UK for a few months?

Her first assignment was to produce a poster for our open day on a Sunday in June. It was an important poster advertising finance deals on all of the machines we were selling. On the Friday evening, I called at Cherie's cottage to collect the artwork. It wasn't quite ready so I returned the following day to be told by Cherie that it still wasn't perfect but that it would be by Monday. I looked at it. It was good enough. Perfect by Monday would have been too late. She understood the message and did a great job from then on. She returned to California with a few months' great experience, and picked up a marketing job instantly.

Good is good enough, perfect is too late

62   I read it in the newspaper, it must be true

One evening, Sue and I were watching 'Tucker: The Man and His Dream', a film starring Jeff Bridges. Jeff was playing Preston Tucker, a failing early motorcar manufacturer being crushed by Ford and other big manufacturers. He was making a superb, unique, distinct car but was having difficulty selling.

He decided to take the afternoon off and took his wife and children to Joe's ice-cream parlour. Preston sat at the counter chatting to Joe while the children were enjoying their ice-creams. Joe talked about an unbelievable way of building houses. It was the early days of prefabricated houses. Preston didn't believe what he was saying, and Joe's famous words were, "I read it in a newspaper, it must be true". For Preston, it was a 'eureka' moment. He realised that getting publicity about his fantastic car could allow him to crack the market.

The more publicity he got, the more sales exploded. He only had short-term success as he was eventually crushed by the bigger manufacturers - but those words left an impression on me, and with JLA's fantastic Clive Hadfield, our superb words guy, we published on a monthly basis, an authoritative magazine for the care industry named 'Caring Standard'.

We included articles by politicians, health experts, insurance experts and finance experts. We carried non-competitive adverts, and put our own adverts on articles. It almost became a bible for the care industry, and people would save every copy as a reference. It must be true, I read it in the newspaper!

We built our brand and increased our sales.

I read it in the newspaper, it must be true

63 Case studies

It is unusual for anyone to get fired for choosing the best in class as a supplier. If you are in a specialist market, the best people to tell you who they think is the best and why, are other people in your market. Therefore as a supplier, your customers are your best credentials.

A referral is where you ask one of your satisfied customers if they are aware of anyone else in their line of business who would be interested in your products and service, and they give you an introduction.

A testimonial is where one of your customers is happy to give you a written recommendation for you to show to prospective customers.

Case studies are where customers are prepared to collaborate with you in preparing a chronicle of how their problems were resolved by you as a supplier.

Each of these provide independent credibility for your business, and if the testimonial is from a recognised, quality business, then it gives even more powerful credibility.

To have the greatest impact, testimonials should be current and relevant.

Our head of words, Clive Hadfield, would travel the length and breadth of the country interviewing customers, to pull together illustrated stories of very happy customers. We had some great case studies with photos of the installation, laundry room and building.

Quotes were given by the management about how they had benefitted from dealing with JLA through:

- cost savings
- improved quality
- hygiene compliance
- superb service

These we would use as PR, but also to arm salesmen with individual stories covering all of our markets.

Case studies

64   Two clicks below slick

I learnt a lot of lessons from John Gregory.

I have known John for 30 years. He was the best route operator ever. He had his own business, Caldwell Gregory, based in Richmond, Virginia, which he sold for a great price about twelve months before JLA was sold.

John taught me how to write proposals to major customers. These included personal references, before and after photographs and lists of all customers, not just a select few. I copied his recommendations and a few months later, took him a copy of JLA's latest proposal. John didn't want to hurt my feelings but I could tell he had doubts. "What's wrong?". "It's too slick, not personal enough. Too many glossy pages. It doesn't look like it has been written for the customer. It needs to be two clicks below slick".

The more the customer can see that the document they are looking at was produced just for them, the more confidence they have that they will receive a personal service from you, and that you have done your research and are well informed about them.

Two clicks below slick

65   Use demographics

Everyone knows that the location of your business is key.

When we were opening launderettes of our own, location was vital, and in the 1980s, when we were advising customers on where to locate their next laundry store, we developed a demographic profile of the ideal location for a store. We questioned 2,000 launderette customers nationally about their usage and, through their postcodes, constructed a profile of self-service, service wash and dry-cleaning customers. This allowed us to have demographic data to map suitable locations for stores. We had to look at traffic flow and parking.

When booking exhibition space, we used the same location rules, always looking for a corner site where customers could approach the stand from four different directions. We looked at entrances, exits and traffic flows in order to choose the best location for our stand.

Use demographics

66 Show your warts

When building new relationships with either individuals or businesses, credibility means everything. So rather than overselling, exaggerating the facts or only telling the good news, it pays to be honest and show your warts. These imperfections show that you are honest and credible and, therefore, the good things that you promote are probably true.

It also gives credibility to what you are saying. If you try to make out that everything is perfect, that you deliver on time every time, you never make any mistakes, it's not credible.

One good example is Sylvie Giangolini, a former Sales Manager at JLA. After we sold JLA, Sylvie appeared for a while to be doing very well but, in her usual style, spoke her mind and, in the opinion of the new management, spoke out of turn. She was devastated to lose her job but picked herself up and applied for a sales management position with a German floor-cleaning equipment supplier I had already left JLA but Sylvie rang me and asked if I would give her a reference. I suggested that I would take a call.

The Managing Director, her prospective employer, rang me. I described Sylvie as lively, passionate, intelligent and motivated but also that she could be a little stroppy and definitely spoke her mind. The MD said, "Well that's a good thing because you don't want yes men". I said, "Absolutely, but it doesn't work in every company". By showing this 'wart', everything else I said became credible. Sylvie got the job and is now Sales Director of that same company.

Show your warts

67   Listen to your customers

You may think you are running the perfect business, but you should never stop asking customers how you can improve.

Why did they become customers in the first place? Because you were providing something they needed and they couldn't find anyone else who was doing it as good as you.

That was then and this is now.

Competition copies you, market conditions change, and customer's expectations of service are raised. What was great six months ago is now commonplace and ordinary. Don't rest on your laurels and wait until your customers drift away because they have found something better.

Regularly ask them if you are still delivering what they need or if you could improve. Listen to them, learn from them and over-deliver.

We carried out a survey of our members at In Touch Networks. The main message was that they wanted a learning and development program. Within weeks we recruited Anne Watson, a successful author of five business books who has great passion and drive. Four weeks later we were producing training and development videos in our own state-of-the-art studio, and it is now the fastest-growing department in the business. It pays to listen to customers.

Listen to your customers

SELLING - WITHOUT IT YOU'RE DEAD

Despite having the greatest business idea, building the best business infrastructure, driving your PR and marketing, without sales you're dead. Get the best salesmen. Nurture them, reward them, hug them and pull them.

68. Sell to your own staff first

69. Find the pain

70. Take credit

71. Two ears and one mouth

72. Build relationships at all levels

73. Under-promise, over-deliver

74. In-house telesales

75. Drive sales, manage margin

76. If you are not going to win, walk away

77. You get further with a smile and a 'gun' than with a smile alone

78. Chase one rabbit

79. Never satisfied, always proud

80. Customers - love them, hug them, grow with them

81. Monitor pipelines

Sell to your own staff first

If your staff and your sales people believe in the product that you are selling, it makes it easy to convince customers that they should deal with you.

For example, American Dryer launched a great new product called 'FSS'. This meant nothing to our customers but it was a great invention to prevent fires occurring in laundry dryers. Clive Hadfield and I spent hours coming up with the right name and brand. The brand we came up with was 'S.A.F.E' which stands for:

Sensor
Activated
Fire
Extinguisher

Our dryers became S.A.F.E dryers, and to demonstrate the safety feature, we connected two dryers - one with the S.A.F.E system and the other without. We staged a fire in both machines. When the two dryers burst into flames, the S.A.F.E system immediately came into action, dowsed the flames and saved the day. The fire in the other machine continued to blaze, but the fire brigade arrived in time to put the fire out. It was great theatre. The salesmen were in awe of this fantastic safety feature and went away believing in the product, which made it easier to sell.

If salesmen are convinced, then customers will be too.

Sell to your own staff first

69 Find the pain

Salesman visits customer. The first thing he needs to know is what problems, what issues, what concerns the customer has. Is it poor service, continuous breakdown of machines, high energy use, poor washability, capacity of equipment?

Find his pain, develop your solution, take the order.

A famous Ralph Daniels quote.

Find the pain

Take credit

The reputation of a business is founded on what it is known for - good or bad. Communication is now almost instantaneous with social media such as Twitter and Facebook. However, unless the customer or staff get to know in the first place what you as a business do well, then you will have no reputation. Every business should take the opportunity to accept credit for the exceptional job it is doing. This is done at every point of contact. If the relationship should ever be strained with any one individual, the more people in that business who understand what a great job you have been doing, the better position you are in to retain it as a customer.

Don't assume that just because you know how good a job is being done, that the customer does. Tell your customers at all levels how good you are.

At JLA, when our engineers visited multiple sites in, for example, a university, and visited several laundry rooms, fixed machines and mopped the floor or helped a student, it would be unlikely that any of the customers, staff or management would see them carry out these tasks. Consequently, they would not leave the campus before explaining to the student services department what a great job they had done.

Use e-mail, send reports, ring the customer. Use every opportunity to say how good you are. However you do it, take credit.

Take credit

71 Two ears and one mouth

Possibly very similar to the f nd the pain rule. We just wa-t to emphasise that God gave us two ears and one mouth. So use them in that proportion. Listen twice as much as you talk. You would be surprised by what you learn and how easy the sale then becomes.

A famous John Laithwaite quote.

Two ears and one mouth

Two ears and one mouth

When selling to an organisation, whether one that employs thousands or just a few, your people need to know as many people in that organisation as possible. For us, engineers needed to know the laundry staff and the maintenance people. Sales needed to know the laundry manager, the head of procurement, head of student services, even the Finance Director. As high as you could go. This would work well if there was any renewal of contracts to be negotiated, as the laundry room was usually off everybody's radar unless there was a problem.

When a contract comes up for renewal, you want to be recommended by the customer's staff at all levels.

The stronger and broader the relationship, the harder it is to break.

Build relationships at all levels

Build relationships at all levels

73   Under-promise, over-deliver

Never make a promise unless you are sure you can honour it. Never say that an Engineer will be with you in four hours if you know that it will take eight. Promise eight and get there in seven. If however, a disaster occurs such as a pile-up on the motorway, ring the customer immediately and communicate that the Engineer is on his way but in some sort of difficulty. Explaining the position to the customer inevitably keeps the customer on your side. We used to do over 500 service calls every day. Inevitably issues occurred. At 3:30pm every day, we would review all promises made and all outstanding service calls. If we felt that we may be letting a small number of customers down, we called and explained that they would be first priority the next day. If any customer had a genuine problem that needed fixing that day, we would find an alternative JLA Engineer and divert him to that emergency.

In bigger organisations, such as national accounts, local authorities or key accounts, the buying decisions are usually made by a number of decision-makers and sponsors. There are, however, usually one or two key people who have been supportive during the decision-making process, and may have been instrumental in you winning the business. They may have spoken out against the incumbent supplier and their supporters in the business.

It is vital therefore that you ensure that your sponsor is supported by you after the decision has been made, and not expose him to criticism for his choice.

Therefore, if there is ever an issue with the customer, the first person to be informed should be your sponsor. He should be told about the issue, what is being done about it and when it will be remedied. This allows him to defend his position as well as yours from others in the organisation who may have an axe to grind.

Under-promise, over-deliver

The great leap forward came in 1982 when I discovered telesales. It didn't exist in the UK so I studied the American model. I visited two or three American companies in London including Dun & Bradstreet. I also met Kathy Lait, an American, UK-based telesales trainer. After a grounding, I started with one telesales person to three Field Sales Managers, and recruited a Head of Telesales, Gillian Orr, from Bupa Membership. She wanted three telesales to one Area Sales Manager. Foolishly, I refused, so, within a month she left. Eventually I compromised and went with one-to-one. I wish I had been braver. The results were spectacular. Appointments were made, sales were closed and figures sky-rocketed. We suddenly became number one in our industry.

Over the years, we tried to outsource telesales. We approached very professional companies but did not find success. Results were very limited due to the use of automatic dialling, scripts and the lack of experience and passion. We believe that telesales is a great way to build relationships with customers, and we could not have achieved it by outsourcing.

In-house telesales

Drive sales, manage margin

Salesmen had clear targets and were driven on an almost daily basis with regular 'phone calls, reviews of appointments, accompanied field visits, regular reforecasts and updates on performance to keep them motivated. To manage margins, we limited their discretion on pricing and gave them what was to be known as 'Traffic Light' price lists. The green price was list price and gave the salesman his maximum commission and the company its best margin. The amber price list was the lowest price that the salesman could offer without consultation. The red price list could not be offered without consultation with Stuart or Richard Logan our Finance Director, and not without the salesman providing a good justification as to why the customer should have that price. This allowed us to manage the margin.

The two most important days of the week were Mondays and Fridays. Each Monday morning, we took a quick look at margins and what sales had been achieved the week before, and asked if there was anything we needed to do to catch up. After a great week, the discussion was how we were going to beat the previous week. The energy in the office on a Friday was electric as we focused on closing orders and hitting our goals. At 5pm, we would have all the information we needed, and could then celebrate the week.

Drive sales, manage margin

76 If you are not going to win, walk away

The institutional market has, over the years, changed its method of procurement to producing tender documents. If those documents are written in a way that the best price always wins, then value for money almost becomes a non-issue. It is therefore important to get close to the influencers of the document, and try to get it written so the customer actually makes the right decision.

If, after reading the tender document, you feel that you don't stand any chance of winning, tell the potential customer that you are not going to tender, and walk away. That way you don't lose.

If you are not going to win, walk away

77 You get further with a smile and a 'gun' than with a smile alone

According to legend, this was said by Al Capone. We don't mean literally give your salesman a gun to threaten your customers. We mean that when you arm them with the best products and customer service, you give them the most powerful 'weapon' so the customer can't say no.

One of our best salesmen, Martin Aston, once told me that our OTEX product was the best 'gun' he had ever had. We had invented and branded OTEX to save money, save time, save energy, be gentler on textiles and kill all superbugs in the wash. OTEX was only available to rent as it required careful installation and a great back-up service. Martin felt that it gave JLA the edge. It gave him the 'gun', and the year we introduced it, around 2004, was our best year for sales growth.

You get further with a smile and a 'gun' than with a smile alone

You get further with a smile and a 'gun'
than with a smile alone

Focus your attention on one goal. One target - but it has to be big enough. In the early 1980s, we were one of seven companies chasing the launderette market. There were several large groups with between 20 and 150 stores. None installed JLA products and despite sending salespeople in, we just wasted time.

Amongst our people, we had Tom Aspden, our Technical Director with over 30 years' experience of managing launderettes but with no sales experience. I asked him to just visit all groups, offer his advice and gently try to get JLA machines in. That was his sole goal. Chase one rabbit. He gained their confidence and slowly we started installing JLA/IPSO/AD machines.

Within two years, we supplied seven of the top ten launderette groups in the UK.

Chase one rabbit

79 Never satisfied, always proud

Drive in any business is so important to becoming a winner. Being a winner is not just about making profit, or being the market leader, it is about how you feel about what you have achieved.

It might be attending an exhibition and being told by the attendees that you have the best stand in the hall. The feeling of getting unsolicited compliments lets you know that you are, in their eyes, doing things right. The pride you feel does not lead you on to be complacent and rest on your laurels, but should drive you on to do greater and better things.

The overriding driver is wherever the initial idea comes from, and despite the fact that you are very proud, never be satisfied.

Never satisfied, always proud

80 Customers - love them, hug them, grow with them

Our business was always about securing and keeping customers for life. Many of our competitors didn't understand customer relationships, wouldn't have regular contact with customers throughout the contract period, and often didn't approach them even when the contract was up for renewal in case the customer decided to go elsewhere.

We understood the power of being seen as a partner with them in their business.

We showed them that we loved them by being proactive in carrying out preventative maintenance visits to reduce the hassle of a breakdown and keep them operating successfully.

We hugged them by being reactive to concerns and offering them innovative solutions to changing operating needs.

We would grow our businesses together because the relationships were so strong they rarely considered going elsewhere.

Our bottom line and turnover grew by a phenomenal 20% each year over a period of 20 years - a large proportion of which came from the existing customers. As they grew, we grew.

Customers - love them, hug them, grow with them

**Customers - love them,
hug them, grow with them**

Many businesses concentrate on bringing orders into the business because, as a first step, you have to get an order before you can deliver it and get paid for it. Getting paid for it is what you're aiming for.

Most companies monitor orders. We monitored pipelines. We wanted to know how strong a pipeline was for the next three to six months. To do this effectively, you had to know your sales people. Some are optimistic, some pessimistic and some realistic. The time to do marketing and to attack the market is when pipelines start to flag.

We had one salesman, a very genuine, lovely person, Graeme Wiltshire, who, when asked what his next week's forecast was, precisely stated £13,345.42 because he already had that order in the bag! Graeme never wanted to disappoint us or let us down, so he only told us what he was certain of You had to know each salesman and how their minds worked, and make adjustments to get a realistic forecast to make the right decisions. In fact, if we could keep the difference between annual orders and annual deliveries down to only a 10% overshoot on orders, we were happy. One week of poor orders was a blip, two weeks was a concern and three weeks was a trend that needed ACTION.

Monitor pipelines

REGNERT 2016

If you stand still, you wither and die. Use new marketing methods. Track website visitors.

82. Never stand still

83. Always ten steps ahead

84. 364 days' service

85. Total care

86. Service on time or we pay you

87. Use technology to win

88. If something is working well, break it and fix it better

89. Reading and writing

90. Never stop learning

Never stand still

In 1973, JLA had one main group of customers who were launderette owners, as that was my background. We were successful at a time of decline in the number of stores operating in the UK. We were removing good machines from poor locations and selling them into good locations that had poor machines. The decline was from a high of 12,000 launderettes in the UK to probably about 2,500 today. We grew the business quite dramatically in the decline but obviously this would not continue forever. Occasionally, a nursing home or a hotel would find out that we existed, contact us and ask us to supply a machine. We supplied it, but it was usually a disaster because for these markets, the customer needed much more expertise.

We had to keep moving, so we upgraded the product and the service we offered. We could satisfy the customers' needs, charge a higher price and make more money. Eventually, this new commercial market became 90% of the business. We innovated with many different offers and products, and developed this into the successful business that we sold in 2010.

If you stand still, someone else will take your market from you.

Never stand still

I always had a page in my working file that was headed 'Ten steps ahead'. This would be reviewed on a bi-monthly basis. First by myself, and if I wasn't completely satisfied that we were at least ten steps ahead of the competition, I would organise a brainstorm with some of JLA's leading managers and sales people to discuss where the competition had caught up and how JLA could move to the next level. Some of the ten steps never changed because the competition never caught up. Service was one of those areas where we were so far ahead of the competition, they didn't even attempt to get anywhere near us.

Telesales was another area where the competition never grasped how we did it.

Steps came from embracing new technology and products and listening to customers' requests to improve their own business operation. This process probably meant that we discarded more ideas than our competitors ever implemented!

Always ten steps ahead

Always ten steps ahead

84   364 days' service

Adding intrigue as well as a great offer to a customer is sure to have a great marketing impact.

JLA offered 364 days' service every year. In first appointments, this always lead to the question, "Why only 364 days?". The answer was that the only day we didn't work was Christmas Day. This gave memorability and credibility, thereby reinforcing the message that 99.9% of the time, we would be available.

So the message is, unlike our competitors, we worked almost every day of the year.

364 days' service

364 days' service

85 Total care

We banned the term 'rental' because rental had negative connotations of only being for people who couldn't afford to buy, or something that you pay for and never own. The reality is that it was good for JLA and it was good for the customer.

Good for the customer

* no capital outlay - leaves you cash to invest in things you can't finance
* peace of mind - no repair bills ever
* no penalty upgrade - when circumstances change, you have 'future-proofed' your laundry
* seven days a week service for 364 days a year
* guaranteed response - we get there on time or we pay you
* fixed price for eight years - no inflation
* removed uncertainty and the risk of ownership - you own the machine - you own the problems
* free installation
* preventative maintenance, reducing any inconvenience due to breakdown
* saved management time, money and hassle - anyone can call to get service, as there was no additional charge

Good for JLA

* long-term visible contractual income
* the chance to have a customer for life

Total care is the term that best describes what the customer got when he signed up to an agreement. It is a great brand that does not need a lot of explaining. Over the years, as the business model was developed and refined, it dealt with all objections that customers came up with when the salesmen were matching what the customer was looking for from its laundry solution provider.

JLA's rental customers were many and varied, but one common theme amongst them was that they could all afford to buy the equipment they rented – or we would not have rented to them in the first place.

Unlike our competitors, who thought that a rental agreement was a form of leasing or finance, we saw it as a supply of an all-inclusive service, supplying a capability of laundering to such a quality required by legislation, and required by their business.

They never owned the equipment and therefore never owned the problems. Customers rented because they wanted to remove the risk of the problems that ownership brought, by paying a fixed monthly payment, and we carried the risk of unforeseen costs.

Total care

I love to admit that this definitely wasn't my idea, it was Stuart's. Ideas were my territory but this was probably JLA's greatest idea and greatest USP.

The competition were too scared to try to catch up. We guaranteed to be on the customers' site within eight working hours. If we were not, the customer could claim £100. If we were four hours late, we communicated with the customer, and if they were unhappy, they could claim £100. If we were more than four hours late, we automatically sent the customer £100 without the need to claim. We proudly published figures every week of how much we had paid to our customers. This was generally in the order of £300-400 per week. This was out of 2,000 service calls, so a pretty good result. This gave credibility to our service offering that meant that we were differentiated from all of our competitors, and even today probably 15 years after we introduced the offer, we are not aware of anyone else that matches this.

The other thing that it did was to make our salesmen know that our service was the best in the world, which made it easy for them then to sell that fantastic service to the customer. It put discipline into our operations team, and we knew that when we sold the business, we sold an amazing service operation.

Service on time or we pay you

87 Use technology to win

Use technology as a tool and not a burden!

Over the years, we made major use of technology with some significant industry firsts.

- mobile communication for all
- integrated, synchronised Customer Relationship Management (CRM) systems between office and field sales
- Engineers' handheld terminals updating job allocation/completion, re-ordering van stocks and invoicing details
- attaching photographs of laundry rooms, taken on mobile 'phones, to CRM records
- vehicle tracking for service and field sales
- integrated systems with data warehousing allowing information to be input once but able to be sliced and diced for analysis
- recording telephone conversations which had resulted in a sales appointment for salesmen, attaching it to the CRM so salesmen could listen to them before they attended the appointment.

We were always interested in using technology to improve our business, and brought in expertise when we needed it. Steve Burrows was a consultant who we brought in on a contract basis to help us to improve our systems. We were so impressed by him that we eventually brought him on board as IT Director.

Steve, as well as helping us to implement what we needed to have to meet commercial requirements, would also make us aware of what developments there were in the market to see if we could gain a commercial advantage from implementing them.

Use technology to win

88   If something is working well, break it and fix it better

Most businesses don't like to change a winning formula. For example, football managers keep a winning team.

Our philosophy was never to be complacent. Even though we were continually breaking sales and profit records, we would look to improve the calibre of sales people, the quality of appointments, and the products we were selling.

When we first brought in key accounts, we had key account sales people who covered an area of the country ie North and South.

It worked well and we picked up many new customers. When we sat down and thought how we could do it better, we broke it. We gave one key account sales person the care industry, solely selling to nursing home groups. We gave our other key account sales person uniforms (for prisons, the armed services, fire service) and they then became experts in their market. We then added housing, hotels and mop-washing. So we went from success to even greater success by changing something that was already working well.

If something is working well, break it and fix it better

If something is working well, break it and fix it better

89 Reading and writing

Business books, periodicals, newspapers and business reports are great ways of learning about new management and business ideas, information and techniques. Not everything in a business book will be new or even relevant to all readers, but there may be pearls of wisdom in there that make a substantial difference to the success of the business. The trick is to find them within the mass of potentially irrelevant detail. How do you do this?

By reading… and writing!

Read the book or document and have a highlighter and a pen ready to flag up great ideas and then make a note of exactly how you would use them in your business.

If it's a newspaper or magazine, tear out the relevant section, write on it the particular point and circulate it around the management team with your comments.

Books should be a learning tool. They are not a possession to be kept locked up, away from a highlighter and pair of hands ready to tear out pages and keep the lessons.

Reading and writing

Every day brings a chance to learn something new, or revise your opinion on something you thought you knew. If it looks interesting and relevant, get involved. Visit other businesses, talk to competitors.

At exhibitions I would always visit competitors' stands, introduce myself and listen to what they had to say. I'd ask their opinions on new developments to see if there was anything I could learn.

In restaurants or bars, if there are lively people who seem interesting and the opportunity arises, I engage with them and am always amazed at what I can learn. Many of my best contacts, relationships and now friends originated from such engagements. As well as learning what the business should be doing, these encounters have taught me what not to do.

One of my best contacts was Richard Lee, who I met in a bar in the Caribbean. I explained my business and he told me he was a consultant. When we got back to the UK, I invited him back to my office, still uncertain of his exact skill set.

I asked him what he could do for my business and he talked about the systems and processes he could put in place to make us more efficient.

He moved a couple of jobs around and arrived a few days later. After two weeks I could see he was transforming the efficiency of our operations team, so I offered him a full-time job as Operations Director and he worked with us for two years. He left us in great shape and returned to consulting.

Sue and I travelled a lot, doing business in Australia, America, Argentina, Brazil, Denmark, and Germany to name a few, and we were always learning new ideas. We spoke to business owners about the way they serviced machines, marketed their products, ran their business. There was always something to learn.

Never stop learning

WHEN THE GOING GETS TOUGH

A business never runs smoothly. You take the wrong turns. Disasters happen.

Be prepared to make tough decisions, and always think that every cloud has a sliver lining. Just look for it.

91. A touch of arrogance, a touch of aggression and a lot of empathy

92. Keeping all the balls in the air

93. If you make a threat, mean it

94. We don't have problems, we have opportunities

95. We are where we are

96. Don't flog dead horses

97. From the ashes of disaster grow the roses of success

98. Brainstorms: think positive then think negative

99. Know your enemies

100. Your fault you pay, our fault we pay

91   A touch of arrogance, a touch of aggression and a lot of empathy

To be a successful leader, I feel you need a touch of arrogance and a touch of aggression, but you also need lots of empathy. When I say a touch of arrogance, I mean enough arrogance to make you confident in your own ability. I think a touch of aggression is necessary for those critical times when you have to fight and win. As in football, you need to win the ball back skillfully and fairly with a little bit of aggression. Finally, you need a lot of empathy in order to understand the needs and issues of the team to put your arrogance and aggression into context and to know what motivates them.

When Stuart and I disagreed about something at JLA, there was no compromise. One view has to dominate and be the final decision. The one who couldn't persuade the other was the one whose idea lost out. It is never personal, it's about what's right for the business.

You can't run a business as a democracy. People follow strong leaders, but leaders have to have compassion. You need different sides to your personality to run a business.

A touch of arrogance, a touch of aggression and a lot of empathy

**A touch of arrogance, a touch
of aggression and a lot of empathy**

92   Keeping all the balls in the air

Everyone knows that in order to keep all the balls in the air, a juggler has to keep them moving through his hands. Otherwise, he will drop the balls.

So it is with a CEO in business. When you start a business often you have to touch each aspect of it to understand whether it is performing as you want it to. However, as the business grows you have to prioritise and delegate to other reliable members of the management team. The job of the CEO is to keep his eye on everything that's happening and make sure all the balls are kept in the air. You can't do everything yourself, but good delegation and timely key performance cashboards are the way you stop the balls being dropped, and keep the business strong.

Keeping all the balls in the air

Keeping all the balls in the air

If you make a threat, mean it

93   If you make a threat, mean it

We never lost a good salesman. However, there was one time when a competitor had been bought by private equity, and the new Managing Director of the company was quite aggressive in trying to head-hunt members of JLA's sales team, offering terms and incentives that were tempting for a few. This caused considerable disruption in the sales force, so Stuart and I called all of them to a meeting and asked them, just like Colonel William Travis in 'The Alamo', "Were they with us or were they not?".

We drew a line in the sand, and those wishing to stay could step over the line and commit themselves to JLA. Those who didn't step over the line could leave. We could have lost our best Sales Manager, but all of the best stepped over the line. The two most tempted weren't our top salesmen. I would say one was average, one below. One decided to leave there and then and the other came to see me in the office. He was a decent guy but if anyone would complain, it was him. I told him to go home and think about it but if he stayed, I wanted his full support in future and no more complaining. He e-mailed me the next day and left.

This could have meant losing some of our best salesmen but as expected, all of the best people stepped over the line.

We made the threat, but we meant it.

If you make a threat, mean it

94 We don't have problems, we have opportunities

In business, we always do everything to the best of our ability and hope that we always get it right – but life isn't like that – things don't always work out the way you expect them to. Lots of people will shout about the good news when it works out better than expected, but when it comes to bad news, they shy away from telling you.

I like to hear about the bad news as soon as it happens, because it is how you deal with bad news that can make the biggest difference to the future. Sometimes the bad news is not as a result of anything that you have done, but it is still up to you to deal with it.

Putting right a problem forces you to re-assess how the problem arose, understand what the consequences are and then find a solution. Finding that right solution will inevitably produce a better outcome for the future. Sometimes it may be an unhappy customer whose expectations haven't been met. By engaging with that customer, you get the opportunity to put things right and end up with a stronger relationship going forward.

Looking at a problem negatively as something that you don't want to address or something that you want to go away - is a problem. Looking at it positively and being prepared to invest in it to get it right for the future is why it is an opportunity.

Ralph Daniels - the practice of positive thinking. Ralph, a great if rather eccentric and sometimes loud American, is a man of complete integrity and passion.

I first met Ralph on safari (on a great American Dryer incentive) in Kenya. Once I got to know him, he became somebody whose company I enjoyed, whose ideas I respected. He has a lot of the same people working for him today as he did 20 years ago. They have great loyalty to him and from him.

In his company, he bans the word 'problem'. That does not mean that he ignores problems, he just views them as opportunities to be in contact with the customer and make all of his customers happy.

Learn from the issues, benefit from them and use them as opportunities. This is the principle we adopted at JLA.

We don't have problems,
we have opportunities

95   **We are where we are**

Don't look back with regret. Only look back to learn from your mistakes and your successes. Never have regrets. Never waste time looking backwards.

So, if you have just lost out to a competitor, find out why. If you can change anything for the next time, change it.

Learn by your mistakes but don't regret them. Constant y move forward, improve your future as you car't change history.

It's not what you lose, it's what you get.

We are where we are

We are where we are

Systems or people. If you make a mistake, try to fix it. Don't carry on ad infinitum. If it is a recruitment mistake, move on, change the person and get it right next time.

We invested in a bespoke CRM (Customer Relationships Management) system and had a software house take our manual card systems and write a CRM computer package based upon it. The new system cost over £100,000 but it was a disaster. It kept losing customer follow-up dates, it slowed the business down, we lost sales, and turnover was decreasing. Stuart was reluctant to scrap it because of the huge investment. We had a heated discussion. We went back to the manual system. Three weeks later, we installed Goldmine, an American off-the-shelf CRM system. It was magic. We used 'Goldmine' successfully for the next ten years.

Don't flog dead horses

Don't flog dead horses

97   From the ashes of disaster grow the roses of success

In 1977, we were selling and renting GE washing machines, starting to be very successful. My supplier ran out of stock and the same week, a boat bringing 200 used machines from Denmark sank.

So I had hardly any stock to sell… DISASTER.

I decided that second-hand machines were too limiting, and having to buy from a UK distributor made for unreliability of supply. So I decided the next day that I needed to be an importer.

I rang Whirlpool who said no, then Maytag - who invited us to New York, and within days, we started importing our own machines. Over the next two years, we became distributors of three top brands.

No ship disaster - therefore no new machines - therefore no successful JLA.

Instead the roses of success.

From the ashes of disaster grow the roses of success

98 Brainstorms: think positive then think negative

When business dipped, or wasn't growing at the usual rate, I would call a spontaneous meeting with the best people who were in the office that day and get their input. There was no agenda. I would think up topics to discuss just before the meeting. Over time, I realised that the meeting achieved far more if, for the first third of the meeting you had everybody thinking with positive thoughts, for the next third everybody thinking negatively, and the last third thinking how to improve the positives, diminish the negatives and develop an action plan.

Brainstorms are all about what could be possible, and not necessarily what will be.

Brainstorms: think positive then think negative

99   Know your enemies

Friends close, enemies closer.

In business, enemies are generally people, organisations or competitors that fear you because they cannot rival your performance or reputation. They therefore often resort to misleading or misrepresenting your business to the outside world.

Know what your competitors or enemies are doing - as with this knowledge and market intelligence, you can manage the relationships better and protect your position. Fear is a wasted emotion that achieves nothing – understand what actions to take and be proactive. Don't be frightened to build a relationship with your enemies, however reserved it might be. The closer you are to them, the more you will find out. Take the fight to them.

Never fear them. Always know what they are doing, and in an ideal world, make them fear you.

Know your enemies

Know your enemies

Every transaction or relationship should be a partnership Not always an equal partnership, but one where each party understands their responsibilities to each other and any other party involved.

In the majority of cases, things will run smoothly and no issues will ensue. However, when there is an issue, the important thing is to get it resolved – particularly if there is a customer at the end of it.

We had sole rights to a great product, American Dryer, a family-owned business. When we started, the President, Martin Slutsky, was heading the company. We had great success with their product, largely due to their innovation, their differentiation and their appeal to the market.

When we had issues such as faulty products, Martin would say, "Our fault, we pay". Sometimes the fault was in the installation, which was our fault, so we paid.

Keeping a customer for life means having enough profit in a deal to put it right if it goes wrong - if it's your fault.

Your fault you pay, our fault we pay

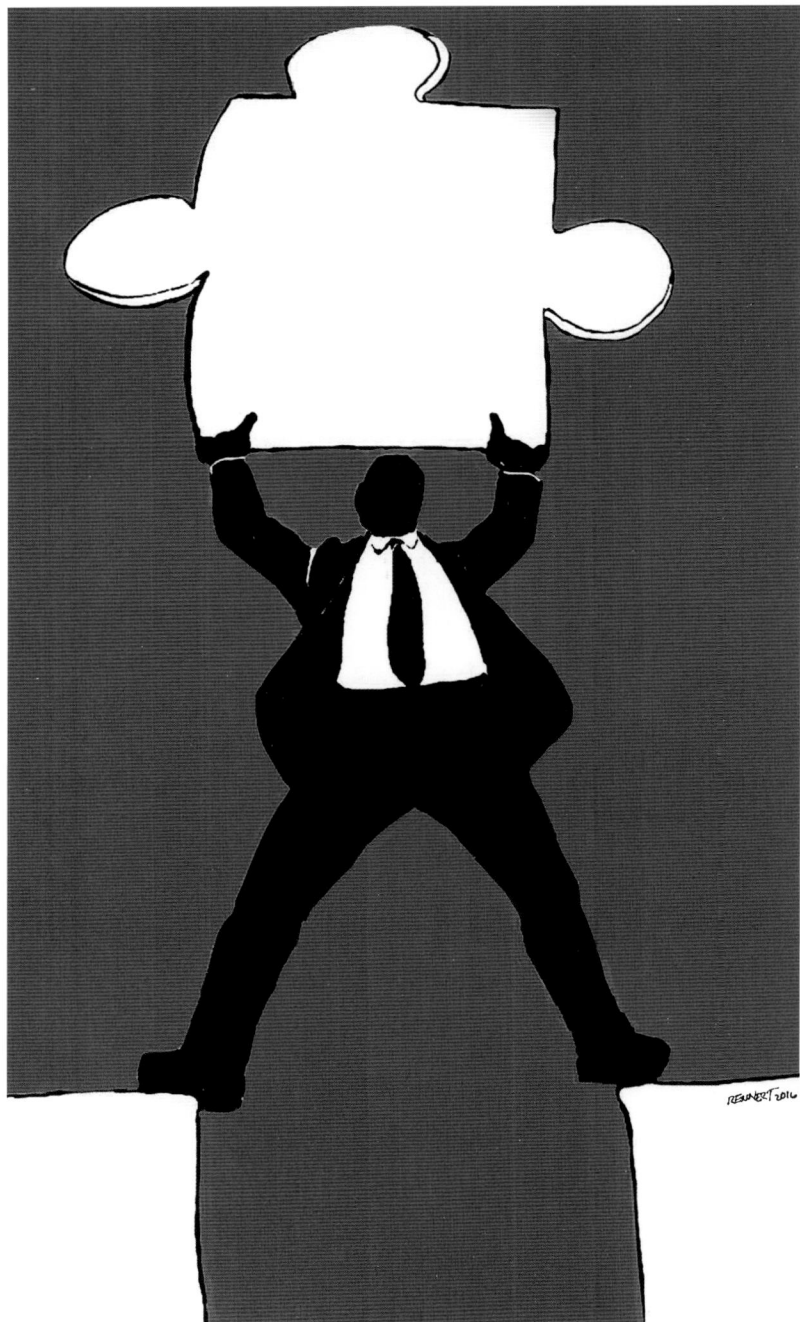

REINERT 2016

THE FINAL PIECE

The final piece of the jigsaw needs you to get away from the business and take a long distance and longer term view.

101. Take time out

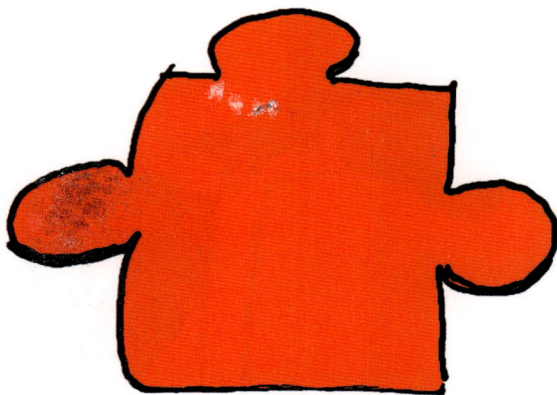

Take time out

101 **Take time out**

Get out of the business, whether it is on holiday, business travel, exhibitions or sitting somewhere with an amazing view. Switch off your phone and your e-mail and clear your mind. You could be on a plane for eight hours, you could be on a beach. You can take a helicopter view of the business.

Don't have any notes or reports, just a blank sheet of paper. Doodle issues, solutions, successes, failures, dangers, opportunities. You'll be amazed by how much you realise you got right and how much you can fix.

Take time out

MEMORIES

We asked a few people to share
their memories of the life and
culture at the original JLA. We have also
added a few from In Touch Networks
These are a few of the responses.

Ying Lin
CEO, Secaide, Shanghai

I still vividly remember when I walked into the big open-plan office, I felt warmth and delight.

I have been to many offices due to my consulting career, and you can just pick up the atmosphere straight away.

The JLA office had this very lively yet organised impression. It's not a dead office, there is no chaos either. Your people are either on a call to customers or talking to each other, professionally yet warm, just like a very delightful symphony. I thought, that's a good office to work in!

However, I was rather shocked with your glass office. I have seen many CEO offices in China. It can be outrageously big and extravagant, isolated from the general staff. In the UK, most of the CEO offices have a wooden frame with frosted glass, at a corner of the open-plan office. But yours was in the middle of the office, and also completely transparent! I thought, wow, you have made your attitude clear! You want to be open and in touch, which is a very positive sign that you are conveying to all your staff.

Sean Smith
CEO, Pethealth Inc.

My thoughts on JLA are very clear.

Take great people, take great care in all you do and magic occurs, lives blossom and careers become a source of pride and inspiration! That's where my mind goes when I hear "JLA". A powerful reminder for us all to "Do the right thing... right".

Pete Thompson
CEO, Invisible Systems Ltd.

It's a pleasure to think back and give a few words of my happy memories of working with the original JLA.

I was proud to be a member of a great team of people. 'People and Passion make it happen' and this was certainly the case at the original JLA.

It was an education, people say you're always learning, but this was more than a learning exercise, it was about being the best and that 'failure was not an option.'

A totally driven company, led by example from the top, a totally open business, best communication, the largest, most successful business in the world in its marketplace, that's what made the original JLA different and a pleasure to work with.

Standards across the whole business were exceptional, resulting in the best in class for customer satisfaction and retention. This made the big difference in my view, the customer always came first, however big or small, they were all equal.

Thinking 'outside of the box' with brilliant 'creative marketing,' generated the business growth and success, that otherwise wouldn't have happened. It made people enthusiastic and hungry to succeed, not just in their own right, but for the business.

Even though when I left the business, nearly 12 years ago, there were about 350 people, a large team, but it had the feeling of a 'small company,' short lines of communication and feeling of a family, friendly togetherness, and absolutely no politics or bureaucracy.

A great, happy, driven atmosphere.

To sum it up, driving a round trip of 180 miles per day for a few years, in rain, snow (the sun rarely shines going up 'Windy Hill') to and from work, usually a 13 or 14-hour day, it must have been a special place to work.

Pete Thompson

It was a sad yet happy day when I left the original JLA but the experience inspired me to set up my own business. Without the education, passion and enthusiasm I had there, I would not have had the confidence 'to have a go'. It's thanks to John and Sue and the team that I am where I am today in a successful business, still having a great, special friendship with John and Sue and others that I worked with there.

A great, special part of my life.

John Harris
A highly successful entrepreneur

My memory is of the people, Bill, Ted, John, Dick, Andrew, Stuart, and of course Sue and yourself. All of these people worked extremely hard but still found time to have enormous fun and time to motivate the people around them to strive for the latest target. They were friends as well as work colleagues and that led to a "mostly" happy environment with each of them willing to put themselves out for the others. The senior people were loyal to the cause and it showed.

The focus on marketing and selling and the intensity and the innovative way in which both of these activities were carried out was also a strong feature of the business. The rivalry of opposing teams as they attempted to win the prize, which was always well worth the effort, was good fun to watch especially in the last day or so of the campaign. I am sure a few teams sailed close to the wind to pull off a victory with the resulting bragging rights until the next time.

The underlying professionalism stands out for me, I don't remember attending a meeting that did not have a specific agenda (written in one of your books John) and the resultant discussion usually explored the topic to the full and was referenced to other information or guidance that was to be taken into account. That professionalism saw the business grow from small beginnings to become the industry leader with superb new offices and a team to match.

The willingness to try new things and to really commit to them i.e. Industrial, Care Homes, Ozone, ensured there was always something new and exciting going on, and all of these ideas ultimately proved to be successful and helped to underline the company's premier position in the marketplace.

Like all businesses, it had its ups and downs but the ups won easily and even the odd down was tackled and overcome with a collective spirit and drive that made the difficulties easier.

All businesses march to a drum-beat and that was given by John and it was always upbeat and positive and filled with a "can do" attitude that was infectious. If there was a target to be reached, support and ideas would be given to those tasked with achieving it and despite my doubts, the target was invariably reached and exceeded.

John Harris

And so my main memory is of the power of motivation, what can be done if people can be motivated by an idea or an individual, in this case I think it was an individual, but either way it resulted in a wonderful success story.

Oh and by the way, I enjoyed every single visit I made to the company and always both learnt something and felt better for the trip.

Ian Greenhill

My memories of the original JLA start way back in 1975 would you believe!!

I remember 'phoning in one day to order machines and to my surprise, John himself answered the telephone. He could not afford a receptionist then. (Just kidding).

We have had a great relationship and friendship since then.

The times we shared at exhibitions and product launches were great both business and pleasure. These were not only in UK but America, Italy, Spain, Belgium, Ireland etc.

The professional approach second to none.

The friendships built up during this time with some of the legends of the industry such as the late "Jovial Giant" John Swailes and Dick Cardis (Champagne Charlie). Ted Hirst, Gerry Margrave, Ernie Hazel just to mention a few.

The difference of the original JLA was that if you had a problem, you could ring up and you would know you could talk to the head of the department whom I knew by name and even the boss himself and get it resolved.

I used to know nearly everyone at JLA. Now I do not know who the boss is or any heads of department.

All my memories of the original JLA are good and I had a great rapport with a well-run, professional company.

Simon Pilling
Bond Dickinson, Leeds

I guess my abiding memory and the thing that really stood out in comparison to other businesses I have advised and been involved in would be the sense of "family" you created.

I remember coming to the party you held when you finally left the business and it was more like being at a family party than a work event.

Through that sense of family, you engendered a true sense of loyalty to both you and Sue, the rest of the management team and the business more generally whereby everyone wanted to contribute in the value creation.

What also came across from stories I have heard was a real sense of wanting to have fun alongside the hard work. I still wish I had been there to see you dive into the river!!

As you say, you built something pretty special!

Alan Glover
CEO, Elenchus Approach Ltd.

The thing for me that stood out about the original JLA was the 'appetite' the vast majority of your people displayed.

This seemed to manifest into work hard/play hard. The other outcome was the number of ventures or enterprises that sprung from that, including my own. I will never forget your words to me – 'Invent your own (psychometric) and we will be your first customer.'

The other aspect I believe was your instinct for marketing; what would work and what wouldn't – you seemed to have honed that over the years.

Lara Wade
Sector Business Development Director, ISS

My first memories of JLA are before I actually joined. I remember the buzz on Friday teatime in The Bridge, when I used to open up and serve the team.

I used to be intrigued how everyone who had worked together all week wanted to continue being together on a Friday night rather than go home. It soon became apparent. It was a family, a family where no matter what had happened during the week it all got laughed about or more often than not celebrated at 5:30pm every Friday. There were so many people from so many places it was bizarre to think that this company on my doorstep just sold washing machines'. Little did I know that I would end up joining the company and spending the first eight years of my career with them. Little did I also know that John Laithwaite would trick me in to a sales role!

The week I finished university (I'd not even graduated) it was the usual Friday teatime shift at The Bridge. John and Sue were in and very casually said, "We need someone organised like you at JLA". Flippantly I replied, "Well I finished uni this week". At this point in my life, when I was just about to turn 21 and having just finished a Public Relations degree it was not part of the master plan to join what I thought was a small family run company within the village I lived, especially one that sold washing machines. I had grand ideas of working in a big city event organising attending glam openings and meeting the rich and famous! But at the time I needed to find a source of income and with the thought of it's best to find a job when you're in a job, I dropped my CV in to Sue. I remember being invited in to meet with John and Dick Cardis. Dick was someone I knew from The Bridge, so he had already given me the heads up of what it was like to work at JLA and the notion that working hard allowed you to play hard and that whilst it may only appear to be washing machines it was so much more.

I remember walking up the glass staircase and seeing the faces from the pub so focused, the screens counting the appointments booked and sales won. Then the glass offices – fish bowls where the Directors sat. I was overwhelmed, not what I had expected, and I can now admit to feeling intimidated.

Lara Wade

The meeting with John and Dick in my opinion was a disaster; I'd specifically told them both that I'd done a PR degree and therefore did not and would not want to do a sales role. In addition I told them that writing was not my strong point. At the time I had no idea what job was available or if at all there was one. But I left that day feeling that there was very little chance I would be asked back.

However, I was, and that was the thing about JLA. If John and his senior team saw something in an individual who could and would add value, they allowed them to, whether there was a position available or not.

Making JLA as successful as it was back then happened because it was truly a people-focused business. If you invested in JLA, JLA would invest in you and the loyalty in both directions created the buzz, the JLA family and ultimately the success. So, I was asked to speak with Louise Webster who I found out later had been told not to mention the word 'sales' to me. At this point, I was 'tricked' into a 'research' role for key accounts. I accepted at the time thinking this will get me through summer. Within my first year, I picked up the award for 'Best Internal Newcomer' but of course still maintained I was not in sales! I soon began internally account managing ISS (my now current employer) and then began winning other accounts in the Facilities Management sector, developing a bespoke solution for mop-washing. Before I knew it, I had a company car, laptop, mobile 'phone and of course a sales target. I had suddenly become everything I didn't want to - but loved it!

Leading to more sales awards, reaching the JLA millionaires club, winning incentives to amazing places such as Dubai and the ability to earn enough bonus and commission that I was able to pay off my student loan by the time I was 27 - a huge achievement.

But more importantly, I met some fantastic people who have and continue to inspire and mentor me in both my personal and professional life. This has of course contributed to my career where last year at the age of 31, I was asked to take on the role of Interim UK Healthcare Sales Director for ISS. I would not have been able to do this without the grounding, knowledge and experience JLA gave me, including the push towards a sales role I was never going to do!

Lara Wade

In this last year, I have on a weekly basis quoted John Laithwaite whereby "good is good enough and perfect is too late" because John always knew that you have to keep moving to keep ahead.

Last week, I started a new adventure at ISS and joined a new sector as Business Development Director, where I am continuing to develop and evolve to meet my personal and professional goals that JLA allowed me to realise at a very, very early age… albeit in sales!

Cameron Tapp
CEO, ClearWater Tech Inc.

After we won John and Dick's confidence in doing business with ClearWater Tech, I assumed it was time to put together a Purchase Agreement. I'm not sure how I was directed to Bob Mills but that's who I started negotiating a contract with. We went back and forth a dozen times negotiating the minute details of our working arrangement. Finally, I think I have it all worked out. Timing was good, I was visiting JLA to move our relationship forward, this was 2003. At some point during the visit, I presented this 20+ page document that I had worked so diligently on, slid it across the table to John.

"What's this?", he says. I reply, "It's the contract I have negotiated with your President". John's expression was priceless. "With my what?". "Your President, Bob Mills". After the laughter subsided and tears were wiped away John says, "Do you mean Dodgy Bob our Parts Manager?".

Much to my dismay I had been diligently negotiating with the wrong guy. John looked at the contract, tossed it in the trash and said that's not how we do business here. He said, we work with people we want to work with… shook my hand and that's the contract we have been using ever since.

Nick Koukourakis
Senior Category Manager, International Sales, Whirlpool Maytag

Here are a few general things I think made JLA special:

- consistent focus on business basics
- stable core management team
- clear decision-making responsibility
- long-term value creation mindset
- stable core values
- recruiting people with a purpose
- passion and spirit of winning

More specifically:

- Fanatical focus on customers: JLA made a point of viewing the world through customers' eyes and as a result focused on how to solve customer problems. Then was not afraid to charge them for the solution.

- Seeking out "real" innovation and capitalising on it. And by innovation, I don't mean just in products, but in everything JLA did, including services and functions. Some examples that come to mind (even if all of them were not all great successes)

1. Aquatex technology and package.
2. Ozone systems for laundries (OTEX).
3. Total Care rental concept for OPL's (On Premise Laundries).
4. Wireless communication technology to enable rental OPL site remote monitoring and report generation.
5. Tracking of service vans and engineers in real time, managing response times.
6. Tracking of incoming telephone traffic down to how many times a telephone rang before it was picked up, measuring team members on this metric.

Nick Koukourakis

- Cultivating long-standing relationships with the "right" mix of supplier brands and products, so that JLA could offer the right product solution to the UK market and for each specific targeted market segment (in other words, Maytag, JLA OEM brand, IPSO, Schultess, all had their place).

- Solid management of sales targets, measurement of results, and accountability expectations.

- Above everything else: Never, ever resting or accepting the status quo. Deeply ingrained philosophy that every day can and should bring new ideas on how to get even better.

Always, everywhere, foster "spirit of winning" and healthy competition: the "league table" screens throughout, the celebrations of winning performances, the acknowledgement of winners, the regular competitions among employee teams with themes (e.g. Formula One teams), the ringing of the bell on a sale closed.

Jean-Baptiste Van Damme
VP Europe, Alliance Laundry Systems, Belgium

Since I joined the laundry industry in 1990, I had two teachers who taught me everything I know. Mike Bohe, the former owner of IPSO, told me everything I had to know about manufacturing commercial laundry equipment, and John Laithwaite taught me everything on how to take the product to the market.

John was and is extremely efficient in this and through his charisma, his market approach and the overall strategy, JLA became by far the largest laundry equipment distributor in the world. Looking back at this great adventure, these are some of the ingredients of the success.

Entrepreneur
John was and is a pure entrepreneur. He will always question himself, his employees, his team, his suppliers. He is a great leader, a good motivator but where he makes the difference and what makes him exceptional is that he hates the comfort zone. If things go well, he will question that and make sure that there will be no self-satisfaction among his team members. He will break that satisfaction to the ground and start all over again. This attitude is very rare and can be found also among exceptional top sport people. Dealing with somebody like this was a continuous challenge as we needed to exceed our own expectations.

Leader
John was and is a natural born leader. People like success, and working for a company as successful as JLA always attracted high skilled people. There was a lot of rotation in personnel (especially in sales and marketing), but even after they were asked to leave JLA, there was still a lot of respect for John as a leader. A good example was the farewell party for John and Sue where John stated with some typical British humour that half of the guests that popped up were fired by him in the past.

Passion
John is passionate and enthusiastic in everything he's doing. A business meeting, a nice dinner in a restaurant, a football game, the same passion will return. If he doesn't see passion in someone, he will not waste his time or spend more time than necessary.

Jean-Baptiste Van Damme

Decisions

John would never leave a meeting without taking a decision. That is why he only wanted to meet decision takers. Somebody that couldn't decide was a loss of time. The consolidation of the industry made it more complicated as a lot of the companies became (too) corporate. In relation to the suppliers, John referred often to Martin Slutsky, the former owner of ADC: "Our fault we pay, your fault you pay". This approach helped us in finding solutions during some difficult negotiations.

Independence

Despite the consolidation of the industry and a lot of pressure, John always stuck to the business model of split suppliers. He was always able to get the best possible products and because of his purchasing power, he always negotiated the best possible price. He was also the first distributor thinking of a kind of personalisation of the product in order to accentuate his independence. As in so many things, also with this he was a trend-setter.

Information

John was the first believer of the great value of information. He travelled continuously around the world looking for information and new ideas. If the idea was good, he would try it in the UK in order to generate new business. Setting up a telesales department and mapping all commercial machines in the UK were ideas that made the difference. He told me many times that the one who has the information will always be two steps ahead of his opponent. Setting up a rental division was most probably the biggest risk that he took but eventually the best decision of his life. Changing an entire industry from sales to rental is doubtless John's biggest achievement.

Family man

If you mention John, you automatically need to mention Sue as well as they always travelled together. Sue and John share the same passion and enthusiasm and many people envied this partnership. You could clearly see their pride talking about the children and grandchildren.

I feel very fortunate to have crossed John's path as meeting someone who drives an industry is very rare. I feel proud and honoured in knowing John and Sue and I'm grateful for all the things I learnt from them.

Alistair Copley
CEO, Wash Station

JLA, my first voyage into the world of washing machines. With John, Sue, Dick and Swailesey. We knew how to make work fun.

- Dynamic team
- Game-changers
- Driven
- Passionate
- Fun
- Full of energy

These are just a few things that set JLA apart from the rest.

I owe my success to John and Sue, I am the person I am today because of my time at JLA. Which taught me about passion and a desire to succeed. I have carried these valuable life lessons into my business, which is now rubbing off on my own team.

In a word, JLA was dynamic.

Angela Cahill
Sales Operations Manager, Reece Safety

I worked at JLA for nearly 20 years and so have lots of memories, only some of which can be repeated!

JLA definitely fitted into the expression "work hard, play hard". On my journey through JLA, I met some great and interesting people, I worked hard, achieved success, hit targets, got promoted, pioneered new markets and products, sold (and rented) a lot of laundry equipment, trained and developed teams of my own, learnt a lot about sales and marketing but most of all, I developed some great friendships, forged a successful career and even met my husband along the way!

JLA was run in a very personal way by John, Sue and Stuart sharing the success and the non-successes of the business to grow the future. It was this personal and open approach that made JLA special. If, in the words of one of the JLA core values, "you've got the balls to do it" then you could flourish and develop new areas of business knowing that you would be supported to achieve success. John, Sue and Stuart not only developed the business but the people within it. Both having a very personal approach to running the business seeking out what motivates you to hit goals and targets. Through this approach a very strong and successful team was developed within JLA giving me the chance to develop and share in the success (and rewards) that our success brought - don't get me wrong it wasn't always easy, I haven't forgotten the legendary JL "feedback" that could also be experienced!

All in all, JLA is a business that I am very proud to have worked in and have on my CV.

June McLean
Owner, Zebra Jewellery

Well, what made JLA different?

It is not one thing that makes JLA different from other companies but a multitude.

When I joined the company aged 21, I had previous experience of a small company and a large company but in both cases, each individual within those companies worked for themselves and had their own agendas. Once I joined JLA, there was always a "we are in it together attitude" and although each and every one of us had our own jobs or targets to reach, we always looked out for each other and would go beyond the necessary to ensure we all reached our goals. To be a member of a "team" that respected one another and were all working towards the same goal was awesome.

Many people came through the doors and within days we all knew if they would "fit in" with that ethos or if they were only interested in themselves. Many did not make it but once a new member showed their commitment, they were embraced and soon became a cog in our team.

The feeling of being part of a great team meant that we were more than happy to socialise with one another, and those social occasions made us even stronger and gave us all some fantastic although sometimes hazy memories!

Of course, the head of that team was John and with his passion to push the company to be "the best no matter what" never wavering it gave us all a very high target to achieve and if we thought we had got there, the bar would be raised. To live up to expectation was very hard for each and every one of us to achieve but try to achieve it we did, and god knows if John thought you were failing you knew it good and proper!

But if you showed your determination to succeed and worked hard, John backed you 100% even if you didn't get to where you wanted, John would recognise your strengths and build on those.

June McLean

During my time at JLA due to the amount of "change" we all experienced, if anyone says we need to change something no matter what it is, I embrace change. Change no longer frightens me. I embrace it as a challenge and that is down to the company and John.

As for stories about JLA, my recollections are always hazy. All I do know is that whether the socialising was through JLA direct, JLA SAS or colleagues organising things privately, a great night was guaranteed. I never remember any violence or nastiness in any event over the 25 years I was part of it, just fun, laughter and joy so thanks for the memories.

Victor Hirmas
CEO, Intertrade, Santiago

What a question! Here are some thoughts:

1) JLA was the reference in the industry for so many distributors in the world that would like to succeed in the laundry equipment distribution industry.

2) JLA was seen as an innovative and creative company. This was a major task.

3) JLA was also seen as a company which worked closely with their customers, hearing them, creating and developing new products and services from their insights.

4) JLA was like a bank - modern, stable and respectful, but also a warm, co-operative and a close company who may give a hand to learn from them.

5) JLA was you John, you Sue, you were the soul of this great company (I can't leave out Stuart from this thought also). A professional company, who had a "great platform" from where all of your employees, trade partners and friends were happy to "be part of". This soul was you guys!

We miss the JLA spirit in the market.

Sylvie Giangolini
UK Sales Director, Hako Machines Ltd

Last time you asked me to put a few memories together it was a lot easier. Four years after leaving it now seems like another life I led! I think the one memory I will hold is the true teamwork we had in the 'good old days'. This is what I try and replicate every day as now Sales Director in my new company. This teamwork meant that whatever happened, whatever was needed and in whatever timescale, everyone pulled together for the benefit of the business and delivered. In all the other companies I have come across, as supplier to or supplier of, I have never seen this again. Truly unique. The experiences I had at JLA (good and bad) have shaped my style and approach as a senior member of a management team of an international company now.

Alessandro Pasini
CEO, Pasvens, Bologna, Italy

I tried to find words to explain what in my mind is still fresh and clear: the first time I came to JLA. As you know, my English is growing in this long time but is still difficult to explain something that is in mind, but I am sure you can understand me. What I feel during my visits to JLA from the beginning to the last time:

Open
Beginning from you, everybody gave me maximum cooperation to learn how they work. What was clear was that it wasn't something strange, but absolutely normal. I feel that this meant that more you are open, the more your mind can catch new ideas.

Passion
Everywhere "breathed" this indefinable passion in everything that was said to me or explained to me.

Respect
Everybody did their best to help each other, colleague or customer.

Organisation
Everybody knew exactly what their task was and everyone was driven.

Desire to win
Everyone did everything that needed to be done to be successful.

Thank you again for your truly important help.

Dave Wheatcroft
Sales Director, In Touch Networks

JLA had a unique way of combining a highly focus-driven business with having lots of fun. The business side was tough, our targets were almost unreachable, deadlines were almost impossible to meet and the pace of change unforgiving but somehow it didn't matter.

Whilst is was always hard work, we created an environment where everyone pulled together towards a common goal, the energy and determination to win overcame any difficulties and we became an amazing business machine.

The business was constantly evolving with new ideas coming on an almost daily basis. This presented its challenges but it kept things fresh. Many of these ideas fell by the wayside but enough were brilliant to transform the business and make JLA dominate its markets sector for decades.

My highlights

In the early nineties, we faced a challenge that our customers didn't have time to visit our offices and showroom. We know that whenever we did get a customer to visit we would always win the business so we invented the "JLA family fun day". We invited our customers along with their whole family to JLA one weekend. The weekend would always have a theme and all the staff would get dressed up in the spirit of the day. We would have entertainers, great food, horse rides, bucking broncos. You name it, we tried it.

These events were loved by our customers and we would have hundreds of visitors over the weekend. Whilst the family were having fun, there was also the serious side. These were amazing sales events and we would often take the equivalent of two or three weeks sales over the weekend and generate hundreds of leads that would keep us busy for months afterwards.

But above all, our customers got to know the business and its great people. We created tremendous loyalty to JLA, and customers became friends who would promote our business across the industry

Dave Wheatcroft
Us against the world

In most industries, there is a leading company that holds the largest market share and is generally regarded as the "market leader".

You then have exceptional businesses that not only lead a sector but totally dominate leaving all other companies in their wake. JLA was one of these companies.

JLA dominated the commercial laundry sector for three decades with great products, innovative marketing campaigns and an amazing sales team. Our competition were united by their begrudging admiration of our next product or initiative.

The industry gossip was always about JLA, there was an insatiable appetite to know what we were doing next, who we'd hired, how they could beat our latest offer. In truth, they were rarely able to compete so they would do everything possible to avoid us.

Working at JLA was like playing football for Manchester United or Real Madrid. You were hated by some, feared by many, but admired by everyone.

Louise Plant
Sales Director, Interserve Support Services

I joined JLA in the summer of 1993 as a young and ambitious Sales Office Manager. The position had been introduced to me by a recruitment consultant and I had attended on a Saturday morning for an interview with vague interest. I can still recall the feeling on leaving that morning that I absolutely wanted to work for JLA – I had been interviewed by John, and his passion and enthusiasm for the business he had built was tangible and highly infectious.

Outperform the market
It wasn't about washing machines – the business focused its efforts on Customer Service. Every day was about delivering exceptional, innovative products that met the needs of our target markets and service delivery that was beyond anything delivered by our competitors.

Ten steps ahead
Meetings were often held where time was taken to discuss and debate ideas where JLA could push further beyond the reaches of our competitors, whether it was products or customer experience.

Employee engagement
Without doubt, whatever your position or role within the business, great efforts were taken to include all employees whether it was an incentive to drive the sales effort or a campaign to gather great ideas. One of the most memorable for me was the STOP campaign where all employees were asked to submit their suggestions for things we should STOP doing and actions we should START to do. Winning ideas were rewarded and recognised across the business. Great sales efforts were also rewarded and recognised. We had some amazing incentives, whether it was flying the winners to Venice for lunch on a Lear Jet, or an extended weekend in Dubai or Chicago. But the brilliant part of these incentives was the way in which all employees were engaged in the objective and the potential reward.

Retention
It was never a surprise to me that many staff were long servers with JLA. I was one of them. The offices were always buzzing with activity.

Louise Plant

Designed to be open plan with department hubs across the space this ensured that departments didn't operate in silos and crucially that department heads, Managers and Directors were 'connected' to the daily business challenges and personnel. It was a truly inclusive organisation.

One of the roles I held at JLA was of National Accounts Sales Manager. We had targeted the residential care home market and at one point, nine of the top ten providers were our customers. This was achieved as JLA took the time to tailor-make solutions to ensure exceptional service delivery. Retention of accounts was very high for this reason and in fact one of our challenges was ensuring that our customers were reminded of our efforts. 'Take credit' was one of our mantras and formed part of our strategic marketing activities to key accounts. If we had attended a vandalised machine or attended on a Bank Holiday, we 'reminded' the customer and took credit.

Fun

As a team we believed in hard work but fun was a huge part of our lives at JLA – whether it was an end of week celebration for sales achieved or one of the sports and social activities. We had annual family days with hog roasts and family activities, as well as the annual Bonfire Night with the most stunning fireworks display - also enjoyed by the surrounding villages! Even our families felt part of JLA.

Friends

Someone once said a job at JLA should be the last one you have as anything else will fall short. I have now moved on and can share that sentiment. My time at JLA was always about new challenges, an overwhelming sense of being part of something exceptional and being best in class. JLA introduced me to friends for life – people who shared the same drive to leave others standing. I've taken all the skills and mantras and now apply them daily in my current position. However, once you've seen the 'magic', everything else seems pale in comparison.

Ian Birch
Principal, Hollings Mill

The Royal Mail always claimed that Wednesday was the best day to receive Direct Mail. So mail shots were diligently despatched second class last thing Friday. The majority of mailers would then arrive on Wednesday as planned.

During this period, JLA heavily utilised Direct Mail for both core business and niche markets.

One niche market was riding schools and stables. Apparently, wet horse blankets are a big issue. We released this particular mailing on Friday as usual and thought no more about it.

Early on Saturday, I received a very excitable telephone call from a normally very laid-back Dick Cardis. He had apparently called in at the office looking for some quiet Saturday time.

"Ian, the 'phones are going mad". The mailing had hit early and there was only him to answer the telephones.

The problem was easily identified. A Royal Mail worker, seeing JLA were now a major customer, decided to give them VIP treatment.

On his own initiative he had decided to treat all JLA second class mail as first class thinking they would appreciate the upgrade.

Sales staff were called in specially!

John Greenwood

If I could choose my working life again and could choose exactly what and where it would be, the chances are I could never replicate the uniqueness of JLA life in the 1980s.

Unique and amazing are two clichéd, overused words nowadays but I can think of no other descriptives that sum up that decade. It was a family atmosphere but at the same time, velvet gloves and iron fists spring to mind, there were no demarcation lines and people pulled together for the common cause and generous rewards, a sort of formal informality really.

There was also the not-to-be-ignored fact that, by and large it was a good, talented team. Needless to say there was a lot of fun to be had and below are just a few snippets of memorable moments in no particular order.

White Lightning opening day, wow! Is this what private industry is about? Bridge tea times, brilliant, will never be recaptured, failures corner, DJ Services auction and catch the greasy pig, family fun days, open days and hog roasts, early 1980's road shows, Whitley Bay, Nottingham, Liverpool, Leyland with Dick and Swailesey.

La Grillade, an Italian in Manchester's Chinatown, Dewsbury canal boat trip, Armenian and Ed Winterbottom. Christmas games knockouts, Christmas draws, Christmas evening in The Bridge, sales meetings at The Griffin.

Ralph Daniels
President and CEO, Daniels Equipment Company Inc.

I clearly recall that every significant JLA business philosophy was created over a beer at The Bridge Inn that always was equated to fun.

John Laithwaite's business plan was implemented in the late 1970s of a rental program and at that time was considered not a cutting-edge model but a bleeding edge concept; "If a salesmen sold a washer, their coat left with it". This bleeding edge concept created the On-Premise Laundry (OPL) industry's prominent cash flow model emulated by many; however, never replicated again. The success of the business model had an underpinning of three ideologies:

- Marketing
- Incentives/Rewards
- Competition with teams within JLA

The three supervisory philosophies of the business plan was mainly successful because of the drive of the JLA's founder John Laithwaite and having being blessed to have his wife Sue next to him. One of Sue's commendable aptitudes was her supernatural ability to employ individuals and that could be blended into the JLA culture.

One of the most important constituents of the business plan was the addition of our friend Dick Cardis in the early 1980s, first a salesmen. John later gave Dick an opportunity to lead the marketing department at JLA. Dick initiated principle changes to OPL marketing at JLA. The high intensity of the Sales Room was momentously assisted with a simple blackboard keeping score – Dick understood that passionate sales people's tenacity was never to be in the lower half of any contest, keeping score was a great motivation.

It would be inappropriate not to mention that Ted Hirst was an additional part of the irreplaceable captivation of the original group.

I was indeed fortunate to have been allied with the JLA group first on personal level and secondarily on a business level.

Martin Goodman
Owner, Wash Angel

I started working for JLA in June 1996 as an Aquatex trainer which meant that whenever an Aquatex system was sold I was one of the trainers who would spend three days on site with the excited owner and staff. The systems were sold initially all over the UK and then worldwide which offered me the chance to travel extensively.

I arrived at a golden time at JLA as Aquatex was the buzz word around the company, and as well as the travelling I attended many of the Clean shows and exhibitions. The exhibitions in particular summed up what JLA was about, the stands and exhibits as well as the sales teams' enthusiasm gave the impression of a stage performance rather than a 'stand' and we always blew the minds of the competitors with our 'show'. The JLA exhibition 'show' didn't end when the exhibition doors closed either. Happy, happy days.

Many years later thanks to JLA, I was given the task of operating the JLA show laundry shop entitled 'Wash Angel'.

The name 'Wash Angel' was John's idea back in 1999 and I was puzzled by his choice of name so I asked John the meaning of 'Wash Angel'. John went on to explain the importance of branding and said the best way to sum up the effectiveness of the name is when customers answer their telephone whilst in the shop they will not say to their husband or wife, "I am at the launderette". They will instead say, "I'm at Wash Angel".

Every time a customer answers their telephone, they ALWAYS announce "I'm at Wash Angel" I have a rye smile although I still don't understand how he figured that out. Genius.

16 years later and I am the proud owner of Wash Angel albeit relocated a stone's throw from the old site at JLA.

I owe all my good fortune to that company and the people that made me feel part of that family.

Carolyn Kirk
Managing Director, Richard Jay Laundry Equipment, Australia

I was fortunate enough to visit JLA a few times after the year 2000 before it was sold. I know my brother also visited in the 1990s and also my parents before that.

My most vivid impression was how good the marketing was and also the internal marketing to the JLA team including promoting competitions. I liked the idea of mailing out an aged care magazine which JLA published, however, that wasn't evident to the reader.

I was also impressed by people's generosity with their time and expertise.

The fact that you built such a successful national and international business from a base in a small village is also remarkable and reflects the importance of inclusive teamwork and having engaged staff. Some of the takeaways that I learned (in no particular order) are:

- Product training needs to be continuous.
- The power of recommendations/casebooks from existing customers.
- Using people's competitiveness to inspire them to be more productive - by competitions and live scoring.
- Providing great facilities.
- The inclusive culture where everyone felt cared for.
- The open-plan office – the first one I had seen that was successfully working.
- Rent to customers for longer (we increased our rental contracts from three years to five years after I visited and we now do them for eight years).

It's been interesting thinking about this and what an impact you and your company had by allowing us to copy your model, both directly and in many subtle ways. This would apply for many companies around the world - JLA's lead has been followed by many!

Cherry Jackson
Managing Partner, MEC

The thing that stood out for me when I first met the team at In Touch Networks was their enthusiasm and drive to make things happen. Meetings were all action-focused and everyone knew what was required of them and when. I knew that no meeting would be wasted time and that I would leave with a clear brief and that if a decision was needed I would get one. Procrastination doesn't exist in their dictionary. The team were focused on driving their business forward and it was great to be involved in such a dynamic and growing business with a clear goal for future growth. Everyone I meet is personable, warm and friendly.

Matthew Jones

Head of Development, In Touch Networks

In Touch Networks has been the most monumental moment in my career. The dynamic and dedication of the team and management makes our competition fear us and our members love us.

We have an incredible work ethic with driven leaders, which is essential in any successful business. This has allowed us to grow at a phenomenal rate by having the right objective, focus and drive.

We have a fantastic team of professionals in the business which is an honour to be a part of. It is a remarkable journey. Since joining the business 15 months ago, I have seen the business and team go from strength to strength.

Matthew Roberts and John have proven to me that anything is possible. We have a simple yet effective goal and direction. The fundamental part of our success is having a clear and structured business model in which our services are bespoke to each and every one of our members.

I am intrigued and excited to see what this incredible journey holds next!

Catherine Holmes
Operations Director, In Touch Networks

From the moment of joining In Touch Networks I felt at home. Even with only six staff there was an incredible energy and determination from day one.

It became apparent to me from the start that Matt Roberts was the main driving force of the energy in the office. The principles in this book run through the core of every plan he makes for our company and the achievement has been phenomenal. No matter what target we set ourselves we not only accomplish it but explode expectations along the way. This will always be one of the best things about this business. The development we make and the commitment to doing this twice as fast as a standard company while still keeping the quality our networks need to succeed is simply amazing.

My main lesson from working with John has been that having the right people in the right roles is a real asset. This way we have driven constant change and adaptability in the company but also continue to provide the best working environment because everyone is valued for who they are. I was taught early on to fit the role to the person, not the person to the role, which is clearly culture that runs throughout In Touch Networks.

The In Touch method is the driving force of adaptable, rapid growth companies that are just as exciting and dynamic to work for as they are successful. This way of working has had a profound effect on my career and the team I have developed.

Acknowledgements

Over nearly 40 years of extraordinary growth, many fun times and occasionally tough times, we were supported by phenomenal people, all out of the ordinary in one way or another. These included staff, customers, contractors, friends and suppliers.

Exceptional staff included Dick Cardis, John Swailes, Ted Hirst, Steve Burrows, Clive Hadfield, Phil Coleman, Jim Monks, Mike Wadsworth, Tom Aspden, Richard Lee, Pete Thompson, Ralph Pickles, Trish Cawley, Francis Ayscough, Martin Welsh, Martin Aston, Vanessa McCall, Malcolm Brook, Nick Smith, John Greenwood, Bill Uttley, Dave Ashton, Dave Hooper, John Cook, Stuart Warrington, June McLean, Alan Turkington, Angela McAndrew, Louise Webster, Tony Thomas, Alistair Copley, Richard Dhama, Andy Scott, Yolanda McGuinness, Dave Wheatcroft, Philippa Gavan, Julian Hirst, too many others to mention. The list is endless.

Exceptional suppliers included the Slutsky family, Jean-Baptiste Van Damme, Eddie Coppeiters, Nick Koukourakis, Ed Winterbottom, Mike Schoeb, Mike Bohe, Claudio Malpensi, Cameron Tapp, Frans Jamry, Walter Darini, Lin Lou Fei and a few more.

Mentors included John Harris, John Gregory, Ralph Daniels, Russ Kool, Dave de Marsh, Doug Fowler, Scott Scarpato, Alan Glover and Victor Hirmas.

Without all of these people and others, we could never have achieved the heady heights of success, and could never have written this book.

Thanks also to Maggie Morris for coordinating the original content of 'In Touch'.

The most important lesson of all: 'Share Your Success'

The skill and talent of our staff has made our business successful, thanks in part to the access they had to great education. Many children do not have this luxury.

We want this to change.

We are dedicated to sharing our success with those in need. In Touch Networks donates £2 from every new membership to the charity, In Touch Futures.

In Touch Futures is the charitable arm to our business, set up in 2016 to alleviate poverty around the world.

So far, we have funded a range of grassroots projects supporting disadvantaged children in the UK, South America and South Africa, and you can help us to do more.

Our ambition is to adopt whole communities, providing them with the resources to educate themselves, feed themselves and find employment.

Unlike other charities, In Touch Futures shares monthly updates with In Touch Futures partners who donate on a regular basis. This feedback allows donors to see exactly who their donation is supporting and how it is being used.

Please support us by becoming an In Touch Futures partner and set up a regular donation via **www.InTouchFutures.com**.

Imagine
if your child
had to sleep in
a wheelbarrow...

IN•TOUCH
FUTURES
Investing in Future Generations

Imagine your grandchild raising their siblings alone...

IN•TOUCH
FUTURES
Investing in Future Generations

Imagine
what a small donation can do...

IN·TOUCH
FUTURES
Investing in Future Generations

Published by	Hollings Mill
Project co-ordinator	Sarah Whittle
Design	Phil Coleman, David Charlton
Illustrations	Jim Rennert

ISBN 978-1-5262-0618-3

9 781526 206183 >

All profits from this book go towards our own charity, In Touch Futures, which aims to improve the futures of disadvantaged children. If you enjoyed this book we would be sincerely grateful if you could leave a review on social media. Thank you.